The Principal as Educator and Leader:

Readings for Professional Development

Educational Research Service

Because research and information make a difference.

Educational Research Service
1001 North Fairfax Street, Suite 500
Alexandria, VA 22314
Tel: 800-791-9308 • Fax: 800-791-9309
Email: ers@ers.org • Web site: www.ers.org
ERS e-Knowledge Portal: http://portal.ers.org

E R S

Educational Research Service is the nonprofit organization serving the research and information needs of the nation's preK-12 education leaders and the public. Founded by the national school management associations, ERS provides quality, objective research and information that enable education leaders to make the most effective school decisions in both day-to-day operations and long-range planning.

ERS Founding Organizations:
American Association of School Administrators
American Association of School Personnel Administrators
Association of School Business Officials International
National Association of Elementary School Principals
National Association of Secondary School Principals
National School Public Relations Association

ERS Executive Staff:
John M. Forsyth, Ph.D., President and Director of Research
Katherine A. Behrens, Chief Operating Officer
Kathleen McLane, Chief Knowledge Officer

Library of Congress Cataloging-in-Publication Data
The principal as educator and leader: readings for professional development/editor, Kathleen McLane.
    p. cm.
ISBN 978-1-931762-65-6
    1. School principals—In-service training—United States. 2. School management and organization—United States. 3. Educational leadership—United States. I. McLane, Kathleen.

LB1738.5.P746 2007
371.2'0120715—dc22   2007046075

Ordering information: Additional copies of *The Principal as Educator and Leader: Readings for Professional Development* may be purchased at the base price of $28.00 (ERS School District Subscriber price: $14.00; ERS Individual Subscriber price: $21.00). Quantity discounts available. Stock No. 0705. ISBN 978-1-931762-65-6.

Order from: Educational Research Service, 1001 North Fairfax Street, Suite 500, Alexandria, VA 22314. Telephone: 800-791-9308. Fax: 800-791-9309. Email: ers@ers.org. Online: www.ers.org. Add the greater of $4.50 or 10% of total purchase price for postage and handling. Phone orders accepted with Visa, MasterCard, or American Express.

Editor: Kathleen McLane

Note: ERS is solely responsible for this publication; no approval or endorsement by ERS founders is implied.

Table of Contents

Foreword

This collection draws from the best of the *ERS Spectrum* principalship literature over the past five years to provide preK-12 principals with a guide to reflective practice. The resource provided here is distinctive in the way it addresses the dual roles of the principal—as instructional leader and managerial leader—in a format that is designed both for individual reflection and growth and for discussion in peer groups and mentoring support.

Each article is followed by a series of questions designed for reflection and discussion, to assist principals, whether new or experienced, in examining their progress and goals in the evolving responsibility of leadership. In each area addressed, principals are asked what the leadership in their schools looks like, and what it should look like. Throughout the book, principals are challenged and guided in becoming the catalyst for those changes in their schools.

The articles are divided into two sections: "Developing Principals for Instructional Leadership: What Good Principals Need to Know" and "Leading by Example: Principals and Managerial Leadership." Throughout, the focus is on the power principals have to improve instruction and student achievement by creating learning communities in which everyone learns—students, teachers, and administrators.

Educational Research Service is proud to present this resource in support of principals everywhere. The goal of our organization is to support you in the critical task of improving the education of all our children and youth.

John M. Forsyth, Ph.D.
President and Director of Research
Educational Research Service

Section One:

Section One:

Developing Principals for Instructional Leadership: What a Good Principal Needs to Know

1 What School Principals Need to Know About Curriculum and Instruction

Gene Bottoms

Educational accountability has changed nearly everything. Super-intendents and local school boards no longer can be satisfied with principals who simply place teachers in the classroom, provide textbooks, and get students to attend school. Increasingly, schools and school leaders are being judged on their progress in teaching most students to the standards that only the "best students" were expected to meet in the past. This means that future school leaders must have in-depth knowledge of curriculum, instruction, and student achievement.

What Do School Leaders Need to Understand about Curriculum and Instruction?

School leaders need to understand the "big ideas" that should be taught in the core curriculum. They do not need to be experts, but they should know enough to determine whether students are being taught the body of knowledge, the understandings and the skills that they are expected to learn in the core curriculum. Also, school leaders must have a grasp of the knowledge, skills and understandings that students need to gain from career/technical courses and electives.

Leaders should know enough about state and national standards in academic courses and elective fields of study (such as fine arts and practical arts) to help teachers identify the most important standards. In other words, leaders need to know that "covering everything and learning nothing" does not work. They need to be able to help teachers identify the things that students should learn in greater depth.

Leaders also need to know how to distinguish between a regular language arts course and a college-preparatory/honors language arts course. Students in college-preparatory courses are expected to do more reading and produce higher-quality work. Leaders should end course leveling and get the faculty to teach most students the key concepts from the college-preparatory curriculum.

Leaders must understand literacy, as well. Reading, writing and speaking are "learning tools" that are essential across the curriculum in academic courses, fine arts courses and the practical arts. Leaders should be able to recognize whether teachers are advancing students' literacy skills and requiring students to use these skills to learn in all courses.

As part of the big picture, leaders need to know what students are supposed to learn and the standards they are supposed to meet in determining whether teachers' exams and assessment guides are appropriate to measure high school and middle-grades work. Leaders need to know enough about assessment to be able to lead reams of teachers who are working together to develop grading guides and common exams. Assessments can help teachers measure their own effectiveness as well as the amount of student learning

What Do School Leaders Need to Know about Instructional Practices?

School leaders should have a working knowledge of research-based, stude centered instruction, such as the Socratic method, project-based learning, cooperative learning, research studies, integration of technology into instructional strategies, and integration of academic and career/technical studies. They need to understand the conditions that will enable teachers to use these methods.

Leaders must be able to recognize whether teachers are using instructional strategies effectively. They should know how to help teachers learn new instructional methods, how to gauge the amount of time it will take for teachers to master new techniques, and how to "network" teachers as they implement new approaches.

Good instruction requires good planning, and leaders need to understand the amount of time it takes to plan effectively. Teachers who are expected to teach higher-level content to more students need time to devise ways to connect what they are asking students to learn with what these students have learned or experience in the past.

School leaders should know enough about teaching and learning to be able to identify teachers who are doing the best job of raising student achievement. Why do students learn more in these teachers' classrooms? Exemplary teachers can deliver "model" lessons and invite other teachers to observe instruction in the classroom.

School leaders must understand the school and classroom conditions that contribute to higher expectations. They need to be able to recognize whether such a "culture" exists in a classroom and to assist teachers (through mentors or other approaches) to expect more of students.

What Do School Leaders Need to Know about Organizing a School for Greater Student Learning?

It may be necessary to create small "learning communities" in which teams of teachers from the core academic subjects and fine arts or practical arts work together to teach a group of students. Leaders should be able to build an organizational structure that will allow teams of teachers to connect what they are teaching and to develop ways to make learning more meaningful to more students. This type of school reorganization, which emphasizes the belief that it is possible to teach more students at a higher level, is particularly effective in low-performing schools. It tends to energize young teachers and create opportunities for new leaders to emerge.

Leaders need to be able to create an organizational structure that promotes higher achievement. They can assign a team leader, a department chairperson or an interdisciplinary leader to head each team of teachers. Team leaders should be teachers who have "bought into" the concepts of higher standards, better teaching and more advanced learning. Principals need to meet continuously with their team leaders to sustain the focus on curriculum, instruction and student learning.

What Do School Leaders Need to Know about Supporting Teachers with Continuous Opportunities for Growth and Development?

Effective leaders provide opportunities for teachers to strengthen their subject-matter knowledge while learning new research-based, student-centered instructional strategies. The best staff development combines content knowledge and instructional methods.

Certain experiences will help teachers change their beliefs about whether students can learn advanced materials. Successful principals arrange for teachers to talk with employers about workplace requirements, to interview former students who had to take remedial courses at colleges and universities, and to visit schools that teach advanced materials to all students. If teachers do not have such experiences, they may not understand the need to change and may not realize that they can teach more students to higher standards. Outside experiences can deepen teachers' subject-matter knowledge and suggest ways to connect classroom activities to the real world.

School leaders must decide that all students will be taught at a higher level. Until then, some teachers will never understand the importance of teaching advanced content to most students. Once the decision is made, principals should make it possible for teachers to learn new instructional strategies designed to involve students in learning.

Successful leaders know the value of providing a "mentor" for each new teacher during the first three years. These leaders assign the "best" teachers as mentors and schedule a series of "learning experiences" for new teachers. Too many high schools—particularly low-performing schools—fail to support and encourage new teachers during their induction period. As a result, teacher turnover at these schools is high.

School leaders must be willing to make follow-up an integral part of staff development. Teams of trained teachers should be allowed to try new strategies, refine their skills and share their knowledge with other teachers.

How Can School Leaders Balance the Pressing Need for Ongoing School Improvement With the Heavy Demands of Non-Instructional Issues and Emergencies?

Many non-instructional situations are the result of low-quality instruction and the school's inability to teach all students equally. Successful principals lead teams composed of assistant principals, team leaders, department heads and others who share a common point of view on raising student achievement. The principal should focus the staff on the important things: teaching challenging content, engaging students in learning and constantly seeking ways to raise achievement. Principals cannot delegate the tasks of creating the vision and maintaining the focus. They must perform the vital function of communicating the school's goals to teachers, students, parents, and the community. School leaders need to know how to delegate effectively and to involve school teams in an overall effort to change what is taught, how it is taught, and what is expected of students.

Leaders need to understand how to use data to promote higher standards and the viewpoint that "effort matters." Leaders who make data-driven decisions can produce powerful changes. Teachers who have access to disaggregated data will have a difficult time arguing with the numbers. However, the leadership preparation programs at many universities contain traditional statistics courses that fail to address data collected from real classrooms or to focus on student assessment, school attendance, dropout rates, college entrance test results, and program evaluation.

Many strategies are available to improve instruction: raising expectations, providing demanding content, planning staff development, forming study groups and promoting team participation in conferences. School leaders must be the "chief learners" and the models for higher performance. It is not enough to know "what works." Leaders must know what is needed now and what will be needed in the future to make continuous improvement.

Gene Bottoms is senior vice president of the Southern Regional Education Board (SREB) and founding director of High Schools That Work. This article is reprinted with permission and may be found on the SREB Web site.

Chapter 1: Questions for Reflection and Discussion

1. How well is the curriculum in your school linked to the requirements of the high-stakes assessments in your state?

    - What do you see as the weakest areas?

    - What, if any, curricular areas do you think have been neglected in the emphasis on raising achievement on high-stakes tests?

    - What can you, as a principal, do to make changes in these areas?

2. Have you found your knowledge of effective instructional practices to be sufficient to evaluate teachers accurately? What would you like to do for your own professional development in learning about the most recent research-based instructional practices?

3. In this chapter, the author says, "The best staff development combines content knowledge and instructional methods." How does this relate to the professional development opportunities made available to your teachers?

4. What has your experience been with providing mentors for new teachers during their first three years of teaching? What changes do you think you need to make in this process? Have you found that attention to mentoring and induction reduces teacher turnover? Does it improve the quality of teaching?

2

Growing and Supporting Instructional Leaders in the New Era of Accountability[1]

Mary Lairon and Bernie Vidales

The Redwood City (Calif.) School District, which comprises a diverse student population, has implemented a major professional development model for principals in order to enhance student achievement at all school sites. The model has three key components: (1) restructuring principal meetings with a primary focus on ongoing professional development, (2) offering mentors to new or struggling principals, and (3) providing ongoing support and monitoring of school sites by district administrations. These efforts focus on site meetings and visitations, classroom observations, and sharing of effective practices.

Enhancing student achievement is a central issue for most, if not all, school districts. In recent years, the California accountability system, in conjunction with the requirements of the federal No Child Left Behind Act, has made districts clearly accountable for this goal. Although student achievement has always been part of Redwood City School District's (RCSD) core mission, achieving that goal was left largely to individual school sites. The district's role was to hire strong principals and provide staff development to teachers in specific areas of focus. Despite these efforts, student achievement levels remained relatively low or stagnant at many schools.

Since Ron Edmonds' (1979) hallmark work on effective schools, research in this area has revealed that a strong instructional leader is the common element of effective schools. District offices were seen more as bureaucrats who needed to get out of the way of these instructional agents of change.Despite the preponderance of evidence identifying the necessity of strong instructional leadership at school sites, little research has been done to answer the question: Are instructional leaders born, or can they be developed? And, if they can be developed: how do we create

---

[1] Article based on "Leaders Learning in Context" by the same authors in *Leadership* (May/June 2003), *32*(5), 16-19.

them; what knowledge base is necessary to support leadership; what skills need to be developed so leaders can exhibit best practices in their schools; and what is the role of the district office in supporting leadership development?

RCSD has asked and attempted to answer these questions, focusing mainly on the role of the district office. Utilizing the findings from current studies that have established the critical role of districts in leading school improvement efforts (Cawelti and Protheroe 2003), the RCSD has created a professional development model combining reality-based experiences, such as focused site visitations, ongoing review of student data, and collaboration between district and school administrators, with research-based discussion and professional development sessions.

Program Overview

The RCSD student population consists of more than 50 percent of students on free or reduced-price lunch and 49 percent English language learners. Over the last five years, significant academic achievement gains have been realized at individual school sites as measured by the California assessment program and local assessment measures. Not surprisingly, the schools making the most impressive and consistent student achievement growth over time were those with strong principals, who are outstanding instructional leaders. Such leaders have the skills and knowledge to align efforts at the school with instructional improvement goals.

During the last three years, the RCSD has created and implemented three synergistic initiatives to develop effective principals. These initiatives have increased the opportunities for principals and district-level administrators to participate in professional development activities and learn from each other. Leaders also have been able to engage in meaningful discussions about instructional practices, as well as encounter real-life examples of leadership actions in evidence at school sites. The initiatives include:

1. Restructuring principal meetings with a primary focus on ongoing professional development.

2. Offering mentors to new or struggling principals and presenting extensive opportunities for principals to learn from each other.

3. Providing ongoing support and monitoring of school sites by district office administration through the continuous review of student achievement data and frequent classroom visits.

At the conclusion of the 2002-2003 school year, after implementing these reforms, all 15 of the district schools met or exceeded established California improvement targets—a first for the RCSD in the seven years of implementing the California accountability system.

Restructuring Principal Meetings

The new format for the monthly principal meetings, which was implemented at all RCSD schools, was based loosely on the practices of District 2 in New York City (Fink and Resnick 2001). For the RCSD meetings, the location as well as the focus moved from the district office to the school sites because current research indicates reform efforts by district and site personnel should be site based, with ongoing professional development focused on what is happening in the classroom (Ragland, Asera, and Johnson 1999). District office business at these gatherings is limited and typically set aside for other monthly district management team meetings.

The impetus for this change began three years ago, when the Santa Cruz New Teacher Center provided a series of intensive trainings on teacher evaluations and conducting quick, effective observations of classroom teachers based on the California Standards for the Teaching Profession. During these sessions, principals and district-level administrators visited classrooms together and shared reflections on what they learned from the visits during the training sessions. The opportunity for observations by peers and colleagues provided valuable feedback for building principals, validating their efforts in instructional leadership and providing a focus for further improvement in the school program. School-based principal meetings and classroom visitations followed by reflection and analysis have become the norm for the ongoing professional development of all instructional leaders.

Though the specific topics addressed at each session might shift from meeting to meeting, the structure and the focus on student achievement in literacy and math remain relatively stable. The host principal usually makes a presentation at the beginning of the meeting, outlining the onsite efforts promoting improved student achievement. These presentations provide insight into the history and nature of the different instructional reforms undertaken by the building principal, including a candid discussion of past and current obstacles and how they were resolved. For example, one successful principal shared how the extensive intervention program at his school, involving both day and after-school sessions, was developed and built. In this school's safety net of services, targeted students were assigned to particular programs according to specific needs diagnosed from careful, intensive reviews of assessment results of students performing below grade level. The presentation included a description of the program several years ago, how the principal built on the strengths of the program and staff, and how he introduced new programs and staff development to fill the identified gaps.

After each presentation, principals from the other sites conduct quick classroom observations, looking for practices relating to the presentations. They then reconvene to debrief and discuss what they saw. Most importantly, during these sessions, principals are able to see the results of leadership actions taken by a peer to improve the instructional focus of his/her school. Principals leave with the knowledge that they can implement similar innovations at their own school sites, and can call someone to help think through both the logistical and big-picture details.

The second half of each principal meeting focuses on a current critical problem and/or issue related to student achievement on which principals share ideas and solutions. Principals generally meet in small groups based on schools that share similar characteristics in grade-level span and type of students served. During a final group discussion, principals often suggest possible next steps, topics for future meetings, and/or ways the district office administration can better support them.

These meetings are a flexible work in progress. As needs evolve and more is learned about effective improvement practices through reviewing a variety of data sources, the meeting structure also may change. For example, in spring 2003, a review and analysis of teacher evaluations revealed administrators varied widely in their assessment of teacher performance: some administrators rated the majority of their teachers at the highest performance level, while others rated most as merely competent. Principals had very different ideas and expectations of what made a truly excellent teacher. After conversations with principals regarding the discrepancies found in the evaluation documents, it was decided additional training and professional development were needed to ensure more consistency in how principals evaluated teacher performance.

Andy Platt, one of the authors of *The Skillful Leader* (Platt et al. 2000), was selected to work with both district and site administrators to enhance their ability to perform evidence-based evaluations. The training process involved several days of professional development, as well as paired and small-group observations of teachers. Training was an eye-opening experience that revealed administrators rate teachers differently using varying criteria. Being able to cite specific examples of evidence from the actual observations has been a foundation on which administrators are being trained to perform evaluations. Such training and development for new principals, along with paired observations, will be an annual component of principal professional development efforts to help ensure a level of consistency in districtwide teacher evaluations.

Although the content and even the structure of the principal meetings change according to need, focusing on onsite school observations and using data to guide meetings continue. The meetings take place primarily at school sites, with time provided for principals to talk with each other. Furthermore, principals' input on meeting goals is encouraged and will remain part of the planning of future sessions and professional development foci.

Mentoring Principals

A natural outgrowth of the trust and respect principals develop for each other through the different site visitations has given rise to two different types of peer mentoring in the district.

"Buddy mentoring," the first and most common form of mentoring, ranges in levels of formality. It usually involves one principal approaching another for support in a specific area or areas. Because principals often encounter similar situations at each school, these mentoring sessions are often problem-solving, group-work sessions that benefit everyone involved. For example, one pair of principals has been meeting to develop systems for monitoring standards-based instruction, student achievement, teacher evaluation, and the relationship among the three. As a result of their conversations, they have developed tools that have been shared and are now being used and modified by other principals in the district. District administration strongly encourages these mentoring relationships, which usually involve meeting at least once a month and may include site visitations based on the feedback desired by the principal initiating the support.

Principals also have begun to regularly utilize the district email system to receive support and get questions answered. Frequent broad queries include requests for schedule suggestions, support for such mundane needs as finding furniture, or more challenging issues such as handling delicate situations involving parents. Principals respond with their suggestions and support, and through these interactions, everyone learns how similar situations are handled at different schools. While most queries are addressed to the general principal audience, others are addressed only to a group of principals with whom history, experience, and support have built trust. These queries might involve questions related to the development of reports for the school board, requests for editing, or suggestions for solutions to problems of a more confidential nature. The use of email allows principals to post their questions to a broad group at one time and allows respondents to reply at their convenience. This technological advance, though criticized as a tool promoting anonymous and impersonal communication, has improved interpersonal relationships among principals and made communication more efficient than the telephone has been able to do.

The second type of peer mentoring is more formal and generally initiated by an assistant superintendent or the district superintendent. It involves pairing an effective principal with a struggling or novice principal. The content of the conversations may be the same as that occurring among the buddy mentors and might include suggestions for developing systems and strategies for handling "administrivia" in order for a principal to become a more effective instructional leader. Site visits, shadowing opportunities, and sharing of effective practices provide the basis for working on other areas. Because the support is generally more specific, the mentoring principal is provided with coaching training in order to facilitate a positive experience for both participants.

Both types of peer mentoring have not only improved the level of professionalism in tackling school site instructional issues, but also have increased the level of collegiality among the building principals. When principals have contact with each other more often than biweekly meetings, and this contact is centered on tackling real situations at respective schools, relationships are strengthened and practice becomes more consistent.

Support from the District Administrators

District office administrators provide direct support to school principals, especially principals new to the district and/or the position. These administrators utilize their own experience as principals to help determine how best to support the administrators at the school sites. Support includes significant help in hiring quality teachers and classified staff, training for site councils and meeting facilitation, the development and writing of annual reports to the school board, site plans and grants for special programs, and dealing with difficult parents, students, and staff.

During the last two years, RCSD office administrators have developed a regular schedule of visitations to school sites, calling on classrooms at least four times a year. The scheduled time involves quick visits usually focusing on a particular subject area or instructional strategy, discussion of assessment data, and ways to help site principals solve problems. District administrators provide another set of eyes and ears with which to evaluate the school program and seek alternative solutions for challenging problems. For example, after visiting classrooms and reviewing reading data at one of the K-8 school sites in September 2002, it was evident there were too many students far below grade level in reading. In response to the evidence and data, the school site administrative team and the district administrator were able to develop a plan requiring the implementation of a new curriculum. The plan included initiating an alternative grouping pattern for students and a teacher training component to better address student needs in reading at the school.

With district support, the new program was implemented in late October, and the majority of students have made excellent progress. For example, 50 out of 55 students advanced at least one level on the California Standards Language Arts test, which shows very significant growth. Once again, the focus is at the site, on the students, and in the classrooms. Student achievement was enhanced by the increased collaborative support and monitoring given by the district administrator. The school's success with this program has been shared with and implemented at other schools seeking better tools to address the needs of older students struggling with reading.

Research also supports the use of student achievement assessments, both formative and summative, to determine the next steps for improvement (Cawelti and Protheroe 2003). Assessment data should be used "diagnostically at frequent intervals by teams of teachers, schools and districts to assess each student's learning and to identify the most effective teaching practices" (Wagner 2003, 28). During the last two years, the RCSD superintendent has worked with his district team to enhance the process of supervising and evaluating principals. The formal meetings between principals and the superintendent have evolved significantly, with a current focus on using student data. A student database developed by the district technology team makes this process more efficient by making accessible the results of ongoing student progress assessments that are integrated with an online report card.

Site administrators are expected to meet with teachers (either individually or in groups) at least three times a year to review student assessment data and discuss the next steps based on the results of the classroom assessments. A specific protocol has been developed to guide principals and teachers in their meetings, focusing on individual student progress as well as overall evaluation of classroom programs. Site administrators then summarize the trends in both the data and the next steps, and present their results with one or two colleagues from other sites to the superintendent and assistant superintendents. The focus of this meeting is not only a time for principals to review results, it also is a time to learn from each other about successful onsite practices to support students and teachers. The process has been extremely valuable in ensuring all players—from teachers to the superintendent—are focused on enhancing student performance throughout the year.

Summary

These three initiatives are examples of what we believe Michael Fullan labels "learning in context" (Fullan 2002), where principals "learn to do the right thing" in the setting where they work. Not only are they observing how other district principals improve student achievement in settings similar to their own, but they are regularly spending time together sharing concerns, ideas, and solutions to real-life problems. Professional development is provided as needs are identified. Furthermore, the district mentoring program involves successful principals working closely with the mentored principal, visiting staff meetings and classrooms, and discussing real concerns and problems at the site. Finally, support of principals by district office administrators is also founded on regular visits to school sites and evaluation/analysis of assessment data collected annually and at each trimester.

These endeavors generally do not require a lot of money to implement, which is an important factor in cost-cutting times. Principals are provided with practical ways to solve problems and institute programs addressing student and staff needs in real-world settings with their peers and district office administrators. The ability of all RCSD administrators to understand and use student achievement and other types of data in order to make meaningful decisions about teachers and program options also has been enhanced.

To ensure the above efforts result in real improvement, a commitment on the part of all district administrators is required to restructure the use of time in order to build and strengthen instructional leaders. The mantra in education for the last decade has been to reduce the isolation of the classroom teacher. Teachers have been encouraged to open their doors, use others as resources, and participate in systematic observation and work analysis programs to improve their instructional practice. We should do the same for principals: encourage them to open their school building doors to peers and colleagues, use each other as resources, and be supported as they implement best instructional practices in their building. The job of the principal is one of the most isolated positions in education. These programs help break down the barriers between administrators, allowing them to develop strong leadership skills together. When this is done well, everyone benefits—especially the students.

References

Cawelti, G., & Protheroe, N. (2003). *Supporting school improvement: Lessons from districts successfully meeting the challenge.* Arlington, VA: Educational Research Service.

Edmonds, R. (October, 1979). Effective schools for the urban poor. *Educational Leadership, 37*(1), 15-24.

Fink, E., & Resnick, L. (April, 2001). Developing principals as instructional leaders. *Phi Delta Kappan, 82*(8), 598-606.

Fullan, M. (May, 2002). The change. *Educational Leadership, 59*(8), 16-20.

Platt, A., Tripp, C., Ogden, W., & Fraser, R. (2000). *The skillful leader: Confronting mediocre teaching.* Acton, MA: Ready About Press.

Ragland, M., Asera, R., & Johnson, J. (1999). *Urgency, responsibility and efficacy: Preliminary findings of a study of high-performing Texas school districts.* Austin, TX: The Charles A. Dana Center, The University of Texas at Austin.

Wagner, T. (November 12, 2003). Beyond testing: The 7 disciplines for strengthening instruction. *Education Week,* 28-30.

Mary Lairon, Ph.D., is assistant superintendent for Redwood City (Calif.) School District (RCSD), and Bernie Vidales is principal of Selby Lane School in the RCSD (enrollment 8,700).

Chapter 2: Questions for Reflection and Discussion

1. The authors base much of the work they describe on the research findings showing that a strong instructional leader is the common element of effective schools. Based on your own experience and the schools in which you have been involved, how do these findings translate into the actual responsibilities and tasks involved in the principalship?

2. How do you think the three components of the professional development model discussed here could be implemented in your district? How do you see the components being brought into practice in your district?

   - Restructuring principal meetings to focus primarily on ongoing professional development

   - Offering mentors to new or struggling principals

   - Providing ongoing support and monitoring of school sites by district administrators

3. How would you answer these questions posed by the authors: How can instructional leaders be developed? What knowledge base is necessary to support leadership? What skills are needed for leaders to model best practices in their schools? And what is the role of the district office in leadership development?

4. What do you see as the training needs for principals to enhance their ability to perform evidence-based teacher evaluations? What are the most difficult aspects of evaluating teacher performance accurately and constructively?

5. What have you found to be the relative merits and disadvantages of "buddy mentoring" and more formal peer mentoring among principals?

3

How Do New Principals Compare With More Experienced Ones in Their Understanding of Student Accountability?

James E. Lyons and John S. Gooden

In 1983, during the administration of President Ronald Reagan, the U. S. Office of Education published *A Nation at Risk* (National Commission on Excellence in Education 1983). This report on the condition of public education in America concluded that a "rising tide of mediocrity" was sweeping across the educational system, which would eventually cause America to lose its competitive edge against other industrialized nations. Although there are scholars such as Berliner, Biddle, and Bracey, among others, who contend that erroneous conclusions were reached in the report, it ushered in a reform era in public education that has continued to the present and likely will affect education for the foreseeable future (Bracey, 1997, Berliner, 1995).

With the publication of *A Nation at Risk* (National Commission on Excellence in Education, 1983), an unprecedented period of school reforms began across America. These reforms, generally categorized as first-wave reforms, dealt primarily with top-down changes from state legislatures. Ornstein notes that nationwide, more than 1,000 state statutes affecting some aspect of school reform were enacted within the seven-year period between 1983 and 1990 (Ornstein, 1991). The approach most frequently taken was the passing of an omnibus education bill by the state legislature that contained a combination of regulations and incentives. Since these state legislatures assumed that schools within their respective states were more alike than different, reform statutes tended to be across the board, or "one size fits all" (Metz, 1988). These mandates primarily called for tougher graduation standards, more testing of students and teachers, longer school days and years, more emphasis on student mastery of the basic skills, more courses in mathematics, science, foreign language, more remedial programs, etc. (Ornstein, 1991). Owens (1998) noted that these regulations facilitated the reach of governmental bureaucracies directly into the classroom by specifying, for example, what textbooks might be used, how many minutes of time should be devoted to instruction, what teaching techniques were to be used, and establishing elaborate systems of examinations and reporting through which compliance could be audited by governmental agencies (Owens). Based upon the speed at which states across the country attempted to reform education by statutes and mandates, it may be concluded that lawmakers sincerely believed that they could legislate educational quality, if not excellence.

Slightly more than 25 years earlier, another incident had also ushered in an era of school reforms. When the Soviets launched Sputnik in 1957 and U.S. policy makers feared they were behind in space exploration, a similar wave of school reforms swept across the American educational landscape immediately thereafter. Principally, the reform efforts that followed emphasized a much stronger curriculum and more effective teaching and learning in mathematics, science, and foreign language. The national goal inherent in these reforms was to overtake and surpass the Soviets' capability in science and technology generally and in space exploration in particular. In contrast, in the "excellence era" launched in 1983, Murphy and Adams contend that the impetus for major educational reforms were driven primarily by economic, social, and political forces (Murphy & Adams, 1998).

First, after hearing that our public schools were not competitive with other first world nations such as West Germany and Japan, the corporate and business community feared that we would lose our ability to compete in the global marketplace and, as a result, the American economy would be threatened. Recognizing that a first-class, competitive workforce is the foundation for a healthy economy, corporate leaders were particularly concerned about the quality of the labor force coming out of America's schools. In response to the heightened interest in public education, President Bush created the New American Schools Development Corporation, which sought to improve the education of future workers by creating higher academic standards (Spring, 1998).

Second, there were social forces that served to provide the impetus to push for excellence in the schools. According to Murphy and Adams, these social forces included changing social dynamics and demographics in America, which included a rising number of minority, poor and less-advantaged students who came from dysfunctional families challenged by unemployment, unwanted pregnancies, alcohol and drug abuse, and violence (Murphy & Adams, 1998). Recognizing this growing category of students, a number of social scientists, academics, policy makers, and policy analysts, for different reasons, saw a need to more effectively address the needs of these students. Some argued that the social cost that society must assume is unduly burdened when a growing underclass leaves school poorly or undereducated and are unable to economically sustain themselves and their offspring. Moreover, when these individuals are unable to obtain regular employment, they are unable to make any appreciable contribution to the local, state, and national economy in terms of enhancing the labor force, paying income taxes, real estate taxes, sales taxes, and contributing to the general welfare of their communities.

Third, Murphy and Adams (1998) contend that political forces also fueled the push for excellence in the schools. The public disenchantment with and cynicism toward government, government agencies, government bureaucracies, and the public sector in general gave rise to the political forces that enveloped public education. Perhaps as a result of the post-Watergate era, which had ushered in mistrust of government officials at the highest level, the public psyche had become disaffected by and suspicious of any function or service provided by government at all levels. Various authors cite specifically how this general skepticism and alienation with governmental officials and services affected public education (Bauman, 1996; Bradley, 1995; Mathews, 1996). The fact that some indicators of educational quality were steadily declining during the '70s served to corroborate the suspected decline in public education. Many critics came to view public education as an ineffective, sluggish monopoly with little incentive to reform. Increasingly, taxpayers came to perceive that they were not receiving a good return for their investment in education, parents became more alarmed about the education their children were receiving, and employers complained that public school graduates lacked the basic skills, work habits, and attitudes needed in the workplace.

As noted above, in the late '70s, the corporate and business community in America was becoming increasing more alarmed with the quality of products being produced and America's inability to successfully develop and produce products on par with Japan and Western European countries. This concern was greatest in the automobile and electronics industries. Peters and Waterman's seminal and widely noted book, *In Search of Excellence,* published in 1982, greatly awakened the national community to the belief that America was quite capable of producing goods, products, and services that equaled or surpassed those of its competitors (Peters & Waterman, 1982). This book profiled and described some of America's most effective companies. Before long, the emphasis on quality began to take hold not only in the private sector but also in public and governmental institutions. Fowler notes that popular writers and politicians had made a connection between the "shoddy" products of U. S. industry and the alleged low quality of education in the United States (Fowler, 2000, p. 118). The argument, she noted, claimed that schools emphasized the lowest common intellectual denominator through a basic-skills curriculum, "dumbed-down" textbooks, and multiple-choice tests that failed to require students to think critically or engage in problem solving. Subsequently, Fowler noted that these students would leave school and enter the workplace unable to make high-quality products or provide high-quality services. Thus, the era of quality was ushered in when forces, primarily external to the educational establishment, began to push for greater educational quality, higher school standards, and eventually educational excellence. As Spring (1998) observes, since the 1980s, the corporate sector has been leading the advocates in favor of establishing national academic standards (17).

Currently, educational excellence has become the clarion call for educators across the country. Some state legislatures have passed what is literally known as Excellent School Acts or other acts closely akin in name. To effect high educational quality and pursue excellence, most policy makers concluded that it was necessary to set high standards that specified what students should know and be able to do as they matriculated through the educational system. Also, they perceived that it was necessary to use standardized tests to measure whether educational goals were being met and to reward success and sanction failure. *Education Week*, in April, 2000, noted that this standards movement has now taken hold as evidenced by the following:

- Every state but Iowa has adopted standards in at least some academic subjects.

- Forty-eight states have testing programs designed, in part, to measure how well students perform on those standards.

- Twenty-one states plan to issue overall ratings of their schools based largely on their students' performance.

- At least 18 states have the authority to close, take over, or overhaul schools that are identified as failing.

- Twenty states now require students to pass a test to receive a diploma and eight more states will require this in three years.

- At least six states have or are planning to introduce high stakes testing wherein student promotion will be tied to test results (Olsen, 2000).

All of the 50 states have now adopted educational reform initiatives that encompass some combination of high standards, challenging content, or school district or school accountability (Goertz & Duffy, 2001). Most frequently, these reforms establish a statewide accountability system and set goals for school districts or individual schools within districts. Additionally, many of the states have identified performance standards and determined how they will measure annual progress toward their achievement. There is wide variation in performance goals and standards among the states; however, there are many common elements of these accountability systems that usually include assessments, standards, performance reporting, and, in most cases, consequences of performance (Goertz & Duffy, 2001). Every state except Iowa has established standards in some subjects, and 44 states have standards in the core academic disciplines (English, math, history, and science). Forty-eight of the states have statewide testing programs, and most have aligned the tests to the standards in at least one subject (Thernstrom, 2000).

Among the states that have comprehensive accountability systems, a few stand at the forefront. These include North Carolina, Texas, Florida, Colorado, Arkansas, Louisiana, Ohio, and Virginia. For example, North Carolina has its "Accountability,

Basics, and local Control (ABC's) Program;" Texas has its "Texas Assessment of Academic Skills (TAAS) Program;" and Virginia has its "Standards of Learning (SOLs) Program." Most of these standardized accountability programs are designed to measure if students learn a predetermined body of knowledge to a pre-determined level of accomplishment. To hold school districts and schools accountable, most of the states have developed a high-stakes testing program to measure student academic achievement. In the majority of cases, there are consequences for school districts, schools, administrators, teachers, and students when significant numbers of students do not reach expected levels of achievement on these tests.

This push for high standards and excellence has become so pervasive that even some of its main proponents have come to worry about the gap between the theory and practice of the "standards-based reform" movement. As Olsen observes in her article in *Education Week,* evidence of a backlash has begun to surface as grassroots organizations in states such as California, Massachusetts, Michigan, and Ohio have encouraged parents to keep their children home on test days (Olsen, 2000, p. 12). In some places, high school students themselves have attempted to boycott tests they were required to take. Many have begun to wonder, notes Olsen, how long politicians can sustain a large gap between the high expectations they have set for students and the percentage of students who can meet these goals.

In 1997, the North Carolina General Assembly directed the State Board of Education to develop a plan to implement high school exit exams, grade-level student proficiency benchmarks, student proficiency benchmarks for academic courses required for admission to constituent institutions of the University of North Carolina, and student proficiency benchmarks for the knowledge and skills necessary to enter the workforce. This initiative, commonly referred to as the ABCs Program, moved accountability from the district to the school level and was designed to more quickly identify students performing below grade effort so that intervention strategies might be timely employed. The program includes Student Accountability Standards called "Gateways" for promotion at grades 3, 5, and 8, which require that students demonstrate grade level performance in reading, writing, and mathematics. High school students are required to pass an exit examination in addition to meeting existing local and state graduation requirements.

The program was specifically designed to essentially end social promotion of students who do not perform at grade level on standardized tests. When students do not initially pass the exams, they are provided two rounds of re-testing and a formal review process. However, principals make all final decisions on promotions. Moreover, students not promoted to the next grade must receive extra help in smaller classes or be provided with additional instructional opportunities. They also may be provided a personalized education plan that outlines the intervention strategies to be undertaken. To support these intervention strategies, North Carolina has spent more than $38 million dollars over the pass three years and will spend an additional $5 million dollars between 2001 and 2003 (Schools, 2001).

Purposes of the Study

Since school principals are the school officials who are most responsible for administering the ABCs program, it is essential that they understand regulations and guidelines that govern the program. Thus, it is crucial that practicing principals and graduates completing principal preparation programs be familiar with these regulations, guidelines, and essential program elements. For these reasons, the authors, both of whom are professors with responsibilities for preparing principals, decided to conduct a study to compare how experienced principals and recent graduates of a principal preparation program compared in terms of their knowledge and understanding of the North Carolina's ABCs Student Accountability Standards Program.

The purposes of this study were fourfold. The first was to compare and contrast any differences that might exist between experienced public school principals (those with three or more years of experience as building-level administrators) and recent graduates of a preparation program for school principals. Specifically, the authors sought to determine if there were differences in the knowledge of these two different groups on the Student Accountability Program in North Carolina, commonly known as the ABCs Program. Second, the study sought to determine if there were differences between the perceptions of these experienced principals and recent graduates regarding the effectiveness of the ABCs Program. Third, through this study, the authors sought to determine the effectiveness of the various modes employed by these two different groups to become familiar with the ABCs Program. Finally, the study was designed to determine if selected demographic factors affected these two disparate groups knowledge, perceptions, and modes of learning (about the ABCs Program) of the two groups.

Methods and Procedures

Descriptive research methodology was employed to conduct this study. The following research questions guided the study:

1. What is the level of knowledge of experienced principals and recent graduates of a preparation program for school administrators?

2. What was the most effective learning mode for experienced principals and recent graduates to learn about North Carolina's student accountability program?

3. What are the perceptions of experienced principals and recent graduates on the effectiveness of the North Carolina's student accountability program?

Using survey methodology, the authors designed a questionnaire that was mailed to a sample of experienced principals and recent graduates of the school administration program at The University of North Carolina at Charlotte. The questionnaire was divided into four parts. Part one asked the respondents to respond to a series of questions that addressed their knowledge about the state's ABCs Student Account-ability Program. Part two asked the respondents to rank the effectiveness of a list of modes for learning about the regulations, guidelines, and elements of the program. Part three asked the respondents to rate their perceptions of the effectiveness of the program. Finally, part four asked the respondents to provide selected demographic information about themselves so that it might be determined if and to what extent they were related to other factors being examined in the study.

A letter explaining the study and asking subjects to participate along with the questionnaire and stamped return envelope was mailed to the 100 experienced principals and 91 recent program graduates in the fall of 2001. The 91 program graduates included all of the students that had earned a master's degree in school administration during the last three years. The 100 principals were randomly se-lected from a database of principals who had served as principals for educational administration students completing administrative internships during the last four years. They were asked to complete the questionnaires in a timely manner and return these to one of the authors within two weeks.

Results

The analysis included 29 recent graduate and 31 experienced principal surveys, which produced an overall return rate of 32 percent. Table 1 describes the partici-pants in the study. Of the recent graduates, most were white (82.8 percent), female (72.4 percent), and had between one and ten years of teaching experience (58.6 percent). Most of the graduates had less than five years of administrative experi-ence and are currently holding administrative positions in elementary schools (51.7 percent). Most of the principals who responded to the survey also were female (82.6 percent), white (69 percent), and had more than six years of teaching experience (74.2 percent); however, 25.8 percent percent indicated that they have been an administrator for less than five years. The majority of the principals (69 percent) also indicated that they are currently serving as elementary principals; 20 percent were middle school principals; and 10 percent were high school principals.

The purpose of the study was to determine if there are any differences between ex-perienced principals' and recent graduates' knowledge and perceptions of the North Carolina's Student Accountability Program. To answer each research question, the data were analyzed using the Independent Samples t-Test. The means, standard deviations, and t-values, and effect sizes are presented in Tables 2 – 4.

The results of the t-Test for the level of knowledge of student accountability standards revealed statistically significant differences between principals and recent graduates in all areas (Table 2). "Knowledge of accountability standards" and "knowl-edge of the Gateways" variables showed the most statistically significant difference at $p < .05$. Both variables have a large effect sizes; 1.16 and 1.02, respectively. Each of the other variables were statistically significant at $p < .01$. However, the variables, "timelines for implementing Gateways" (ES = .64) and "knowledge of standards applicable to exceptional children" (ES = .57), had a medium effect size.

When analyzing the data, the t-Test revealed a statistical difference for the "administrative internship" variable at the $p <. 05$ level. Although the effect size for this variable is large, the comparison probably is not relevant because most did not participate in an administrative internship. The same conclusion could be drawn for the "formal university coursework" variable, which showed a statistically significant difference at the $p < .05$ level and had a ES of .70. The results also revealed a statistical significance for the "LEA's professional development activities" and "overall effectiveness of any accountability training" variables at the $p < .05$ level. Both variables have a large effect size.

Table 4 arrays the data for the perceptions of the student accountability program category. The results revealed that there was a significant difference for the "fairness of standards to regular education students" variable at the $p < .05$ level, and it had a medium effect size of .78. The variable, "effectiveness of standards for more able students," was significant at the $p < .05$ and had a medium effect size (0.74).

Discussion

North Carolina principals are at the heart of the accountability movement because it is their responsibility to make each of the component pieces work. As the findings from this study suggest, principals are keeping abreast of the accountability policies, procedures, and timelines mandated by the state. This is imperative because principals have the ultimate responsibility for curriculum implementation, student assessment, and student promotion and retention. Although recent graduates' ratings of their level of knowledge of the various accountability standards were lower than the principals, it is evident from their responses that they see its importance. In each of the knowledge areas of the accountability program addressed in this study, there was a statistically significant difference between the mean rating of the experienced principals and the recent graduates. In particular, principals are more knowledgeable than graduates in each of the following areas:

- accountability standards;

- gateways (grades) in which students are assessed;

- options for students who do not pass the gateway examinations;

- subject areas in which students are tested at Gateways; and

- principals' responsibilities for accountability standards.

Table 1. Demographics

	Recent Graduates (n=29)		Experienced Principals (n-31)	
	n	%	n	%
Gender				
Females	21	72.4	25	80.6
Males	8	27.8	6	19.4
Race				
White	24	82.8	21	67.7
Black	5	17.2	10	32.3
Teaching Experience				
0-5 years	5	17.2	3	9.7
6-10 years	12	41.4	9	29.0
11-15 years	7	24.1	7	22.6
15+ years	5	17.2	8	22.6
Administrative Experience				
0-5 years	29	100	8	25.8
6-10 years	—	—	2	22.6
11-15 years	—	—	7	22.6
15+ years	—	—	9	29.0
School Level				
Elementary	15	51.7	22	69
Middle School	8	27.6	6	20
High School	6	20.7	4	10.3
Highest Degree Held				
Masters	27	93.1	18	58.1
Educational Specialist	2	3.4	8	25.8
Doctoral	—	—	5	16.1

Recent graduates' lower ratings could possibly be because most of the recent graduates are currently employed as assistant principals and do not have the ultimate responsibility for their school's accountability results. Moreover, they are unlikely to have had the level of professional development that principals have been provided about the state's accountability program.

To keep informed about this constantly changing accountability environment and processes, the data indicated that principals are gaining most of their knowledge from district level professional development, independent reading and research, and state sponsored professional development, respectively. On the other hand, as a

Table 2. Level of Knowledge of Student Accountability Standards

	Recent Graduates		Experienced Principals			
	Mean	Standard Deviation	Mean	Standard Deviation	t-Test	Effect[1] Size
Knowledge of accountability standards	3.28	0.65	3.86	0.35	4.28**	1.16
Knowledge of Gateways	3.28	0.70	3.83	0.38	3.71**	1.02
Timelines for implementing Gateways	3.10	0.82	3.48	0.51	-2.12*	0.57
Knowledge of subjects areas assessed for Gateways	3.24	0.79	3.69	0.47	-2.63*	0.71
Knowledge of standards applicable to exceptional children	2.90	0.82	3.31	0.47	-2.36*	0.64
Aware of options for those who do not pass Gateways	3.14	0.92	3.66	0.48	-2.69*	0.74|
Aware of principal's responsibilities for standards	3.38	0.78	3.83	0.38	-2.79*	0.78

[1]Effect size equals the difference of the means divided by the standard deviation.
* = p< .05   ** = p< .01

vehicle for learning about the state's accountability program, recent graduates rated their formal university coursework low. However, in terms of effectiveness, they rated, in rank order, administrative internship, independent reading and research, and district sponsored professional development. This is an interesting phenomenon because it demonstrates how students have compartmentalized their university experiences since their independent research projects and their administrative internships are an extension of their formal coursework.

The majority of the principals rated their formal coursework and administrative internship very low as modes for learning about the state accountability program. Since the program was not enacted by the state legislature until 1997, it might logically be concluded that it was not possible to learn about the programs through these vehicles when they were completing their administrator preparation programs.

Recent graduates and principals did not view social promotion or retention as effective methods to achieve student excellence. This is an interesting finding

Table 3. Learning Mode

	Recent Graduates		Experienced Principals			
	Mean	Standard Deviation	Mean	Standard Deviation	t-Test	Effect[1] Size
Independent reading and research	2.93	0.70	3.24	0.58	1.84	0.48
Administrative internship	3.17	0.89	1.48	0.94	6.94**	1.85
Formal university coursework	2.10	0.82	1.48	0.94	2.66*	0.70
State sponsored professional development	2.31	0.93	2.69	1.07	-1.44	0.38
LEA's professional development activities	2.86	0.88	3.52	0.63	-3.27*	0.87
Overall effectiveness of any accountability training	3.00	0.63	3.10	0.56	2.12*	0.17

[1]Effect size equals the difference of the means divided by the standard deviation.
* = p< .05   ** = p< .01

because school districts must do one or the other when promotion or retention is being considered. This finding confirms that administrators, like the rest of the educational community, are still grappling with the effectiveness of both of these practices in terms of their effects on student achievement. While both groups strongly disagreed that social promotion is an effective tool to achieve educational excellence, they disagreed virtually as strongly that retention is an effective means to achieve educational excellence.

Although principals strongly indicated that the accountability standards were effective and fair to both regular (average) and more able students, recent graduates provided much lower ratings in each of these areas. Both principals and recent graduates indicated that it was in the exceptional children's area that the accountability standards were least effective. Recent changes in North Carolina's policies and procedures pertaining to exceptional students are very confusing to the educational community; therefore, there is a need for more professional development about accountability in areas pertaining to children with special needs.

Recent graduates and principals also differed in their assessment of the effectiveness of the learning modes available for learning about the accountability program. Principals rated highest the professional development that was provided by the school district, while recent graduates rated their administrative internships as the most effective vehicle for gaining knowledge about the program. However, both

Table 4. Perceptions of the Student Accountability Program

	Recent Graduates		Experienced Principals			
	Mean	Standard Deviation	Mean	Standard Deviation	t-Test	Effect[1] Size
Effectiveness of standards	2.57	0.74	2.93	0.70	1.88	0.50
Fairness of standards to regular education students	2.55	0.69	3.10	0.72	2.98**	0.78
Effectiveness of standards for exceptional students	1.86	0.69	2.00	1.00	-0.61	0.17
Effectiveness of standards for more able students	2.43	0.92	3.07	0.80	-2.81*	0.74
Social promotion is an effective method to achieve excellence.	1.32	0.55	1.43	0.57	-0.72	0.20
Retention is an effective method to achieve excellence.	1.59	0.57	1.55	0.57	0.23	0.07

[1]Effect size equals the difference of the means divided by the standard deviation.
* = p< .05   ** = p< .01

groups rated their own independent reading and research as the second most effective vehicle for learning about the program.

In summary, the findings of this study indicate that in North Carolina principals and recent graduates differ significantly based upon their knowledge of their state's accountability program. Principals in this study were significantly more knowledgeable than recent educational administration program graduates on the standards, implementation timelines, student assessment practices, and subject areas tested at specified grade levels or Gateways.

Conclusions and Recommendations

Several conclusions can be drawn from this study. First, it confirms that principals and recent graduates are knowledgeable about the North Carolina Accountability Standards. This is primarily due to the efforts of local and state educational agencies to provide professional development activities. However, the two group's levels of knowledge differ significantly. Principals in this study were significantly more knowledgeable than recent educational administration program graduates on the standards, implementation timelines, student assessment practices, and subject areas tested at specified grade levels. Local and state educational officials and educational leadership programs must continue these efforts and provide additional training, especially to beginning school administrators who indicated that they are not as proficient in this area. More specifically, they must provide additional accountability training in the exceptional children's area.

Second, given the findings of this study, it appears that principals perceive that they are quite knowledgeable of North Carolina's ABCs Accountability Program. However, recent graduates reported that they did not perceive that they were thoroughly knowledgeable of the program. For this reason, it is recommended that preparation programs in the state place more emphasis on the statutes, policies, guidelines, and procedures under which the state's accountability program operates. This could be achieved through the use of case studies, research projects, presentations by state and local education officials, on-line tutorials, etc.

Third, both principals and recent graduates indicated that neither social promotion nor retention is an effective method to effect student academic success, a position that is also shared by many educators across the nation. Given this dilemma, additional research and study should be devoted to the efficacy of retention and promotion of students who have not demonstrated academic achievement at expected levels, as should research about other alternatives. School administrators should begin to express their views and concerns to legislators and policymakers about these promotion and retention policies since they have the ultimate responsibility for their implementation.

Fourth, both groups also differed on their assessment of the effectiveness of the learning modes available for learning about the state accountability program. Principals rated highest the professional development that was provided by their school district, while recent graduates rated their administrative internships as the most effective vehicle for gaining knowledge about the program. However, both groups rated their own independent reading and research as the second most effective vehicle for learning about the program.

Finally, the findings did indicate that both principals and recent graduates, most of whom are assistant principals, indicated that they were generally knowledgeable of the statutes, policies, regulations, and procedures that pertain to the state's accountability program. Given the front line leadership responsibilities that they have for providing oversight and supervision for the program at the school building level, it is comforting to know that they deem themselves sufficiently prepared to discharge their important responsibilities.

References

Bauman, P. C. (1996). Governing education in an anti-government environment. *Journal of School Leadership, 6.*

Bracey, G. W. (1997). *Setting the record straight: Responses to misconceptions about public education in the United States.* Alexandria, Va.: Association for Supervision and Curriculum Development.

Bradley, A. (1995). Public backing for schools is called tenuous. *Education Week* (October 1995), pp. 1,13.

Fowler, F. C. (2000). *Policy studies for educational leaders: An introduction.* Upper Saddle River, NJ: Prentice-Hall, Inc.

Goertz, M. E., & Duffy, M. C. (2001). All over the map. *Education Week* (April 2001).

Mathews, F. D. (1996). *Is there a public for public schools?* (1st ed.). Dayton, Ohio: Kettering Foundation Press.

Metz, M. H. (1988). Some missing elements in the educational reform movement. *Educational Administration Quarterly, 24*, pp. 446-460.

Murphy, J., Adams, J., & Jacob E. (1998). Reforming American's schools 1980-2000. *Journal of Educational Administration, 36*(5), pp. 426-444.

National Commission on Excellence in Education. (1983). *A nation at risk.* Washington, DC: Government Printing Office.

Olsen, L. (2000). Worries of a standards "backlash" grow. *Education Week* (April 2000), pp. 1,12-13.

Ornstein, A. C. (1991). Reforming American schools: The role of the States. *NASSP Bulletin, 75*(537).

Owens, R. G. (1998). *Organizational behavior in education* (6th ed.). Boston: Allyn and Bacon.

Peters, T. J., & Waterman, R. H. (1982). *In search of excellence: Lessons from America's best-run companies* (1st ed.). New York: Harper & Row.

Schools, N. C. P. (2001). *North Carolina's student accountability standards receive national attention.* Retrieved September 25, 2001.

Spring, J. (1998). *Conflict of interest: The politics of American education.* New York: Longman Publishing Group.

Thernstrom, A. (2000). Testing and its enemies. *National Review, 52*(17).

James E. Lyons, Ph.D., is a professor in the Department of Educational Administration, Research & Technology at the University of North Carolina at Charlotte. John S. Gooden, Ed.D., is an associate professor in the Educational Leadership, Policy and Law Program at Alabama State University. An earlier version of this article was presented at the Southern Regional Council on Educational Administration Annual Conference, Jacksonville, Fla., 2001.

Chapter 3: Questions for Reflection and Discussion

1. What differences have you observed between the knowledge and skills of new principals and those with several years of experience? What, in your view, could improve this learning process?

2. The authors found the following types of professional development to be ranked the highest in learning about state accountability programs:

    *   District-level professional development

    *   Independent reading and research

    *   State-sponsored professional development

    Based on your own experience, what role does each of the 3 sources play in advancing the knowledge and skills of a principal? Are there other resources or activities that you have as helpful or more helpful?

3. If you had an administrative internship in your graduate program, did you find that it played a key role in your preparation? More or less than your coursework?

4. If you were responsible for developing the professional development opportunities for principals in your school district, what would you do differently?

4

Leading to Learn: Knowledge Management Enables Administrators to Excel as Instructional Leaders

David E. Weischadle

The article discusses knowledge management as a means of changing the way administrators carry out their role as instructional leaders. Knowledge management utilizes many concepts from learning organizations, encourages the formation of communities of practice, and employs best practices as a means of leading others to improve learning.

Instead of focusing on test scores and other lag indicators, the article suggests the use of Kaplan and Horton's "balance scorecard," which uses leading indicators to change educators' mindsets.

Education journals and periodicals are replete with articles on issues relating to the No Child Left Behind Act. Since the law was passed in 2002, K-12 education professionals have spent hours pondering its implementation relative to student success rates, annual progress, and school failure. At the heart of this thinking is testing. Schools are evaluated on how well students do on a test or series of tests.

Emerging is a clear mindset. If you ask a realtor the essence of property value, he or she automatically responds, "Location, location, location!" Similarly, far too many educators answer the question of school value or quality with, "Test scores, test scores, test scores!"

Test scores and other simplistic measurements have driven education for many years. In a recent study of testing in three states, researchers reported that perceived negative effects include "reduced instructional creativity, increased preparation for tests, a focus on breadth rather than depth of content coverage, and a curriculum sequence and pace that were inappropriate for some students" (Clark et al. 2003, 9).

Tests seem to preoccupy decision makers at all levels. But educators have begun to challenge the trend. One of the most promising alternatives is called "knowledge management." Knowledge management is particularly attractive because of its relationship to both individual and group learning, and its collaborative, inclusive nature.

Changing the Mindset

State assessments, standardized tests, Scholastic Aptitude Tests (SATs) and high-stakes testing are dominant forces in education today. Educational Testing Service, the College Board, the Psychological Corporation, McGraw-Hill, and Harcourt are multi-billion-dollar test providers. The impact of testing on schools is amplified by the amount of time many teachers and administrators devote to test preparation, administration, and analysis. Similarly, class schedules, teaching time, and professional development have focused on test-taking skills, time on task, and teaching to the tests.

In particular, school administrators find themselves leading their schools in such a way that decisions relating to time, money, and staffing are reflected in test results. This dependence on test scores to measure student success may even be misleading. Good student test scores, in fact, give many principals status and other benefits, but they have only marginal impact on student achievement. Other very constructive administrative practices in schools with poor test scores prove that much of what traditional school administrators do simply will not influence test scores.

Standardized scores, grade equivalents, and percentiles have become the statistics of education. In the academic arena, they are the "stats" that tell parents, taxpayers, and the community at large how well they are doing. As we check the economy using such statistics as Gross National Product, unemployment levels, and productivity rates, so, too, we review SAT scores, pre- and post-test results, and passing rates to determine school success. Is it possible we are missing something?

Consider a recent development in the sports world. One of the most interesting bestsellers to hit the bookstores was *Moneyball: The Art of Winning an Unfair Game* by Michael Lewis (2003). The book, and the people about whom Lewis writes, challenged many time-honored descriptions of baseball success.

For a century, we have evaluated baseball players, teams and the game itself on batting averages, runs batted in (RBIs), and earned run averages (ERAs). But while these statistics are important, they may be only one set of significant measures. More importantly, they may not be the best statistics to use.

Moneyball challenges the accepted practice of spending large sums of money on players with high batting averages, large numbers of RBIs, and low ERAs. Lewis lauds examples of great success (e.g., the Oakland Athletics) using players with low salaries and modest traditional statistics, but with other evidence of worth shown by alternative statistics.

In addressing the traditional mindset, Lewis says, "The standard statistics were not merely inadequate; they lied. And the lies they told led the people who ran major league baseball teams to misjudge their players, and mismanage their game" (2003, 67).

The revolution in re-thinking baseball statistics started with a few individuals who began to think outside the box. Bill James (1996) and other analysts spent more than two decades trying to convince owners and managers that walks and extra base hits were as important as homeruns and strikeouts. James was trying to create opportunities for others to make baseball "so clear and interesting that it provoked a lot of intelligent people to join the conversation." (Lewis 2003, 78).

A Different Approach

While educators, like baseball officials, may be looking at the wrong statistics, we nonetheless need some form of measurement. The fact that our administrative models depend on measuring, benchmarking, or assessing tells us we need to consider carefully whether we are using statistics, or if statistics are using us.

Alternatives such as knowledge management open up the process and allow leaders to re-think the basis of decision making and problem solving. Key components of knowledge management are collaborating, managing teams, sharing information, employing best practices, and measuring performance.

What really makes knowledge management attractive to schools is its emphasis on organizational learning. Knowledge management can meld the management of schools with the work of schools—reading, writing, mathematics, and thinking, to mention a few. Data are a lot of numbers, facts, and letters; information is the grouping of data into somewhat meaningful patterns. Knowledge, however, is what takes this material to a new level. As Ahmed, Lim and Loh note:

> Knowledge involves the individual combining his or her experience, skills, intuition, ideas, judgments, context, motivations, and interpretations. It involves integrating elements of both thinking and doing (2003, 9).

In effect, while information is dormant, knowledge is dynamic and active. Clearly, organizations have been able to greatly expand their data and information bases, but they have been slow to put that material into play, solving problems and making decisions.

Increasingly, American businesses have found that the work people do in their offices and factories has changed. While some are still preoccupied by the service economy concept, it is just a brief stop on the way to a knowledge economy. As Stewart points out, "The flavor (of work) is unmistakable. An ever-growing percentage of people are 'knowledge workers': Information and knowledge are both the raw material of their labor and its product" (1997, 41).

As the "knowledge worker" becomes dominant, so too is "knowledge content of all work" becoming the way of life. In fact, more than ever, the "work" of the workplace is similar to students' "work" in school.

When Peter Senge (1990) introduced "the learning organization" concept in his book *The Fifth Discipline*, he was making an obvious statement to schools. If students must learn to use data and information, then teachers and administrators must also learn to use data and information to operate the schools. Students and teachers all are knowledge workers. It follows, then, that the principal should also be one! Once again, Ahmed, Lim, and Loh effectively describe the substantive relationship between learning and knowledge:

> In our view learning involves the action(s) of using existing insight or knowledge to produce new insight and knowledge. Knowledge is a state of understanding (explicit and tacit) which helps guide the form and shape of action(s). Learning and knowledge therefore mutually reinforce each other in a cycle (2003, 17).

What knowledge management really does is establish a foundation for a different culture that most principals and teachers are not familiar with. It seems no matter how we seek to change education, it adopts a bureaucratic and hierarchical structure. School reform is adopted by a state agency, a board of education, or a superintendent, and passed down to principals and teachers to implement.

In contrast, knowledge management argues against such an infusion process. At the heart of knowledge management is "human capital"; that is, the people who make up the organization. For schools, these people are students, teachers, principals, parents, and community members. Human capital comprises the skills, talents, values, and attitudes of people with a role in their destiny. To encourage this energy, the administration needs to re-think how people work, how they relate to each other, and what they value.

Leading to Learn

While it is increasingly clear that administrative behavior needs to evolve into a leadership model that encourages student learning, it is unclear how this will occur. Knowledge management adds new dimensions to administrative thinking and may well be able to enhance student achievement. Knowledge management forces leaders to focus on staff learning as well as student learning. It follows that staff will be instrumental in the mission of the organization (student achievement) if there is an effective means to guide staff to achieve it. Knowledge management seeks to harness the ideas and talents of the teacher—a true knowledge worker—to ensure sharing and communication, to collaborate and work together, to set up measurement processes to assess work, and to identify and use the work of others that has been proven to be "best practices."

At the same time, the knowledge manager or principal must encourage his or her teachers to see students as knowledge workers as well. In doing so, the principal functions as a true information gatekeeper. In organizations such as a school (knowledge organization), the knowledge worker (teacher) must be a focal point of attention. Such an approach, however, means a different management strategy:

> From the knowledge worker's perspective, management's role is like that of a coach; to help establish common goals, to receive work, offer constructive criticism, and supply or orchestrate resources. Like a coach, management also focuses the knowledge worker's attention on the work at hand, in part by handling logistics, resource allocation, and conducting activities that could distract or even demoralize the knowledge worker (Bergeron 2002, 78).

In effect, adopting a knowledge management approach changes the organization's culture, or at least begins the process. The principal and the teacher are facilitators of learning. Principals encourage teachers; principals and teachers both encourage students. Nonetheless, it is the principal who has the prime responsibility to create a culture in which ideas, talents, skills, and abilities are nurtured, supported, recognized, and in some way, rewarded.

While these activities can be allowed to happen naturally, it is beneficial to create an environment that will encourage the formation of what has become known as "communities of practice."

Such communities are a mix of traditional group dynamics and networking, as well as the synergy of knowledge acquisition. Very informally, communities of practice bring together people of similar interests who meet whenever they want or need to. They discuss their activities, share thoughts about their work, and listen to each other's ideas. The principal, as the knowledge manager, assists with scheduling planning time, finding a place for the community to meet, and providing assistance to make the work flow. Such communities provide the teacher/knowledge worker with a challenging and supportive group of colleagues who share a drive to improve student learning.

Forming the basis for such communities is the search for "best practices"; that is, those approaches or techniques that work in the classroom. Meeting in these communities leads to discussion, and discussion leads to action.

This process focuses on a key aspect of knowledge management: the sharing of knowledge, which leads to action. For knowledge management to work, it is not sufficient to have knowledge; it is essential also to share it, to use it, and to generate new knowledge. In effect, the community of practice is an incubator of innovation. Crucial to the process is that the organization benefits from using the best practices identified by the communities. Tried in the classroom, documented by other teachers, and printed for all to use, these "best practices" can be replicated, refined and applied. As Wenger noted,

> .... [L]earning and the generation of knowledge in communities of practice occur when people participate in problem solving and share not only the knowledge necessary to solve the problems, but also insights into the doing itself (in Ardichvili 2002, 94).

Once again, it is important to emphasize the importance of sharing knowledge and disseminating information. This sharing is what generates a creative environment of taking existing knowledge and reshaping it to create more knowledge. It also creates the framework to determine if what is being posed as knowledge, or a "best practice," is truly effective.

In effect, sharing knowledge is the very basis of organizational learning that will discover effective teaching techniques and promising learning strategies. But even more important, this human exchange of ideas "builds social capital, trust, morale, and culture." (Steward 2002, 202). When these ingredients are present, the principal will find that creating an effective school is possible. Learning is not only the outcome, it is also the process to achieve it.

As a result, traditional measurements of student progress as a means of assessing school values and worth are limited and perhaps harmful. Bukowitz and Williams state, " Assessment at its worst becomes an impediment to change because it ceases to provide information about what is really important to the organization" (1999, 218).

This comment is similar to what Lewis advocated in *Moneyball*. Not surprisingly, knowledge managers have begun searching for new approaches that provide more appropriate techniques to assess how well their organizations are doing.

Sensing these emerging issues, Robert Kaplan and David Horton (1992) devised the concept of the "balanced scorecard.". The resulting system seeks to enlarge the assessment process and integrate it into the organization's work planning and implementation. It is easily adaptable to schools.

Balanced Scorecard

The balanced scorecard initially sought to shift decision makers away from depending solely on a financial indicator to assess how well the organization was

Indicator Areas	Lag Indicators	Lead Indicators
Learning and growth of organization	Turnover rates Retention rates	Amount (hours) of staff training projected and completed in subject area New skills acquired in teaching Participation in a "community of practice"
Student progress	Standardized test scores Absentee rates	New subjects being studied Portfolio development—goals and achievement
Stakeholders interests	Parental participation levels Voter participation in school board election	Ideas in use suggested by parents Activities to increase support from the community
Financial concerns	Per-pupil expenditure Record of budget passage by voters	Cost/benefit of immediate activities to improve reading and other subjects Amount of money invested in new learning activities

functioning. Even more important was the dependence on what are called "lag indicators," or measures of things that have already happened. Dependence on such indicators is like driving a car looking out the back window.

What is needed are real-time measures, or future-based indicators. Such a shift means that managers and principals need to carefully consider the measures they use to make and implement plans. In addition, they need to shift attention to internal areas and develop indicators that place demands on day-to-day activities. While there are benefits to understanding past successes and problems, it is more important to direct current policy.

The current emphasis on test scores is clearly a dependence on what could be described as a "lag indicator." Test scores are always dated by the time schools receive them. Schools need "lead indicators" associated with the total scope of the school organization. A lead indicator seeks to focus on activities that will set direction and answer immediate questions on how well they were done. The indicators become a map for a growing organization.

For schools, the scope would include the following four indicator areas, listed in order of priority:

* *Learning and growth of organizations*—What does the faculty and staff need to learn and improve on in order to achieve the school's vision?

- *Student progress*—How does the school need to relate to students, parents, and the community?

- *Stakeholder interest*—How does the school need to function to meet the issues of students, parents, and the community?

- *Financial concerns*—How well does the school allocate financial resources to meet students' needs?

These four areas interact to achieve the school's mission. The key is to assess indicators in all four areas and recognize the importance of each area, as well as the significance of all four together. No one set of indicators is more important than any other; hence the word "balanced."

Where to Begin

As with most issues related to schools, introducing change begins with the principal. No other professional in the school has the responsibility, or stands to benefit as much. Clearly, the knowledge manager/principal needs to understand how people of all ages learn. He or she needs to see how learning takes place informally and incidentally; how young and old use their competence, skill, and knowledge in the school's work; and how a culture of sharing knowledge leads to organizational growth and development.

Three key components are essential to knowledge management: trust, tolerance, and reward (Figallo and Rhine 2002). Participants of a knowledge management organization look to the knowledge manager to provide such a culture. Working in such a climate, where ideas are appreciated, where honest mistakes can be made without fear, and where one can share in the success and satisfaction of the group is the ideal place for knowledge workers to thrive.

If knowledge management is to succeed, the principal must become the chief knowledge manager. In effect, the principal, along with the teachers and students, need to form a community of learners and transform it into a community of achievers.

References

Ahmed, P., Lim, K., & Loh, A. (2002). *Learning through knowledge management*. Oxford: Butterworth Heinemann.

Ardichvili, A. (2002). The role of human resource development in transitioning from technology-focused to people-centered knowledge management. In C. Sleezer, T. Wentling, & R. Cude (Eds.), *Human resource development and information technology* (pp. 89-104). Boston: Kluwer Academic Publishers.

Bergeron, B. (2003). *Essentials of knowledge management*. New York: John Wiley & Sons.

Bukowitz, W. and Williams, R. (1999). *The knowledge management fieldbook*. London: Financial Times/Prentice Hall.

Clarke, M., Shore, A., Rhoades, K., Abrams, L., Miao, J., and Li, J. (2003). *State-mandated testing programs and teaching and learning*. (Report issued January 2003.) Boston: National Board on Educational Testing and Public Policy.

Figallo, C. and Rhine, N. (2002). *Building the knowledge management network*. New York: Wiley Technology Publishing.

James, B. (1996). *Major league handbook 1996*. Skokie, IL: STATS, Inc.

Kaplan, R. and Norton, D. (1992, January-February). The balanced scorecard —measures that drive performance. *Harvard Business Review*, 71-79.

Lewis, M. (2003). *Moneyball: The art of winning an unfair game*. New York: W.W. Norton & Co.

Senge, P. (1990). *The fifth discipline*. New York: Doubleday/Currency.

Steward, T. (1997). *Intellectual capital: The new wealth of organizations*. New York: Doubleday/Currency.

Stewart, T. (2001). *The wealth of knowledge*. New York: Doubleday/Currency.

Wenger, E. (1998). *Communities of practice: Learning, measuring, and identity*. Cambridge: Cambridge University Press.

David E. Weischadle, Ed.D. is professor of education and program coordinator, graduate programs in educational administration at Montclair State University, Montclair, N.J.

Chapter 4: Questions for Reflection and Discussion

1. The authors cite the following techniques as key components of knowledge management:
   • Collaboration
   • Managing teams
   • Sharing information
   • Using best practices
   • Measuring performance

   What do you see as the role of each of these components in a successful school? Are they helpful in counteracting the current emphasis on high-stakes testing?

2. On p. 37, the authors draw a distinction among data, information, and knowledge. How do you see these distinctions in what schools do today, and how do you think a principal can influence this?

3. The authors propose the role of the principal as the leader of a group of knowledge workers comprising students, teachers, and parents. How would this change what you do as principal or how you do it?

4. How do you think this shift in thinking and behavior would affect the culture of your school?

5. What factors do you see as inhibiting the kinds of changes described in this article?

5 Improving Instruction Through Schoolwide Professional Development: Effects of the Data-on-Enacted-Curriculum Model

Rolf K. Blank, John Smithson, Andrew Porter, Diana Nunnaley, and Eric Osthoff

The instructional improvement model Data on Enacted Curriculum was tested with an experimental design using randomized place-based trials. The improvement model is based on using data on instructional practices and achievement to guide professional development and decisions to refocus on instruction. The model was tested in 50 U.S. middle schools in five large urban districts, with half of the schools in each district randomly assigned to receive the two-year treatment. Each school formed an improvement leadership team of five to seven members, including teachers, subject specialists, and at least one administrator. Teams received professional development on data analysis and instructional leadership and then the teams provided training and technical assistance to all math and science teachers in their school. The central premise of the treatment model is to provide teachers with data on their instructional practices and student achievement, to teach them how to use that data to identify weaknesses and gaps in instruction compared with state standards, and to focus school-level professional development on needed curriculum content and classroom practices. After a two-year period of implementing the improvement model, the analysis of change in instruction showed significant effects of the model. The longitudinal analysis of instruction before and after treatment showed math teachers in treatment schools had significant improvement in alignment of instruction with standards compared with teachers in control schools, and the math teachers on the leader teams showed significantly greater gains than all other teachers.

Since the effective schools movement of the 1970s and '80s (Edmonds 1979), initiatives to improve the quality of public schooling in the United States have continued to build on the idea of improving education through schoolwide programs that involve all education staff, including administrators and teachers. Currently, education leaders are being presented with several models for improving the effectiveness of classroom instruction and increasing student achievement that advocate for better use of data to guide decisions about instruction. Schoolwide models for instructional improvement such as those advocated by Marzano (2003), Garmston and Wellman (1999), Schmoker (2002), Love (2001), Black and Wiliam (1998), and Fullan (2002) have several common themes or components to their models: (a) a schoolwide improvement design that involves school leadership and most/all instructional staff; (b) an ongoing process for instructional improvement involving administrators and teachers, including time scheduled for staff to work together and time for teacher development of content knowledge and subject-specific pedagogy; (c) structured activities for training staff to analyze data on student performance and data on the educational environment that explains performance differences; and (d) use of disaggregated data to identify learning problems and gaps between expected and actual performance and frequent use of data as a formative evaluation tool to guide instructional decisions and plans. These characteristics of schoolwide improvement models are also found in the designs for Comprehensive School Reform that were promoted and implemented starting in the 1990s and supported under Title I federal education funding (Desimone 2002; Tushnet, Flaherty, and Smith 2004; Borman et al. 2002; Cross 2004).

Another type of application of data can now be added to the "data-driven" models for instructional improvement. The Data on Enacted Curriculum (DEC) model for improvement uses data on instructional practices and enacted curriculum taught in classrooms to offer educators an additional rich source of information to provide formative evaluation data and direct feedback to teachers. The model also guides leaders in planning and decisions about professional development and instructional improvement initiatives. A key feature of the model is the capacity to analyze gaps and weaknesses of instruction in relation to standards, assessments, and improvement goals.

This paper reports on results from testing this school-based model for teacher professional development and instructional improvement. The DEC model is based on prior research and development of Porter, Smithson, and others (Porter 2002; Porter and Smithson 2001; Porter et al. 1993; Gamoran et al. 1997; Blank, Porter, and Smithson 2001). The Porter-Smithson research focused on methods of quantifying data on classroom instructional practices and instructional content. Subsequent development and wide field testing of survey- and data-reporting instruments have resulted in a set of practical data tools that can be applied in a school-based professional development model (Blank et al. 2004). The DEC model provides leaders and teachers with needed knowledge and skills, as well as the necessary data, to make informed decisions about the content areas of instruction that should be strengthened to improve student learning. The model has a strong research base, is cost effective, and demonstrates results in improving instructional practices in a targeted subject area.

Many of the recent data-driven models for instructional improvement focus on using achievement data. One recent model emphasizing instructional data is the lesson study model adapted from research with Japanese schools (Lewis, Perry, and Murata 2006) and the video-based instructional practices data from the Trends in International Mathematics and Science Study (TIMSS) research of Stigler and Hiebert (1997). The lesson study approach provides in-depth analysis of a small number of teachers and classrooms, along with extensive feedback and guidance to focus improvement of specific teachers' knowledge and practice. By comparison, the DEC model emphasizes the collection of critical indicators of instructional practices and content for a whole year's curriculum and the use of Web-based surveys to analyze instruction across many teachers, schools, and districts. (For a review of other data-based improvement models and Web links, see the Council of Chief State School Officers/Appalachian Educational Laboratory [2001] online tool at http://www.ael.org/dbdm/.)

Components of the DEC Model

The DEC model for improving instruction begins with collecting and reporting data to teachers on their instructional practices and then organizing and delivering an 18-month process of training, technical assistance, and ongoing support to staff for improving instructional effectiveness based on their own school-level analyses. The DEC model is based on five advances in education research and development of data tools:

(a) improved quality and efficiency of survey methods of data collection on instructional practices, both pedagogy and content (and ensuring validity);

(b) research findings documenting the characteristics of effective professional development;

(c) procedures for analyzing the content of curriculum materials, including content standards, assessments, and textbooks that provide the basis for measuring content alignment;

(d) development of collaborative strategies for school staff to work together on raising student achievement; and

(e) computer software programs that allow for analysis of complex instructional data and for graphic portrayals of survey practices data and content alignment data; these software-generated graphics provide a key vehicle for encouraging educator group analysis, reflection, and discussion of instructional improvement.

Based on these advances in research and application of research tools, the Council of Chief State School Officers (CCSSO) was awarded a grant from the National Science Foundation (NSF) in 2000 to conduct an experimental design study that would test the DEC model for instructional improvement (CCSSO 2002). The study design carried out from 2001 to 2004 consisted of place-based randomized trials, with middle schools in large urban districts randomly assigned to the treatment or control condition (Porter et al. 2005). The study team tested the hypothesis that the DEC model would significantly improve instruction in math and science at the middle grades level, with the dependent variable being the measured improvement in degree of alignment between instructional practices being taught and the state content standards for the grade level and subject (Blank et al. 2004). The study addressed two key research questions:

(1) To what extent does the DEC model for professional development improve the alignment of instruction in mathematics and science?

(2) What are the conditions for implementation of the model that explain positive effects?

Surveys of Enacted Curriculum

A first key step in the model is collecting and reporting baseline data on the instructional practices carried out in classrooms over the prior year. The Surveys of Enacted Curriculum (SEC) for math and science were designed and field tested with NSF support in the 1990s (see Blank, Porter, and Smithson 2001; Porter and Smithson 2001), and these surveys are now used in schools in 16 states. (To review the surveys and a summary of current projects, see CCSSO [2003] online access at http://www.SECsurvey.org.) The surveys, designed for use with math and science teachers, report data on pedagogical practices used in a year-long course, homework, student grouping, classroom assessment strategies, technology use, teachers' opinions and beliefs about teaching, professional development, and the content teachers cover. The items are grouped into a dozen scales for purposes of reporting and analysis.

The SEC uses a two-dimensional grid for collecting information about the subject content taught in classrooms. The first dimension lists topics (in mathematics or science). Mathematics content areas are (a) number sense, (b) measurement, (c) data analysis/probability/statistics, (d) algebraic concepts, (e) geometric concepts, and (f) instructional technology. Each of these general content areas is broken down into a dozen or so specific topics. For example, under geometric concepts are specific topics such as angles, symmetry, and theorem. The second dimension of the grid relates to expectations for students (referred to here as "cognitive demand"). Categories of cognitive demand in mathematics are (a) memorize facts, definitions, formulas; (b) perform procedures; (c) demonstrate understanding of mathematical ideas; (d) conjecture, analyze, prove; and (e) solve non-routine problems/make connections.

(For more on the research and development of the surveys, see Porter 2002; Blank, Porter, and Smithson 2001.)

Research on Effective Professional Development

The DEC model is consistent with the common findings of a number of research studies over the past decade that established the characteristics of effective professional development, especially in math and science (Cohen and Hill 2001; Desimone et al. 2002; Weiss et al. 2000; Kennedy 1998; Garet et al. 2001; Loucks-Horsley et al. 1998). From his review of the set of studies addressing math and science professional development, Elmore (2002) concluded there is a "consensus from research" about designing and implementing professional development. The research has shown effective professional development (a) engages participants in active learning, giving them the opportunity to construct their own knowledge; (b) is designed for groups of participants (e.g., a team of teachers or all teachers in a given grade from a school); (c) is coherent (i.e., tailored to the teachers' level of experience and aligned with the content standards, assessments, and other policy instruments of the system within which the teachers teach); (d) focuses on the content of instruction, and especially knowledge of how students learn that content; and (e) is sustained over time (in contrast to one-shot workshops).

The DEC professional development model builds on the findings from these studies by focusing professional development activities on the curriculum taught in the participating schools and classrooms, and the model involves the teachers and staff as colleagues working together on improving their skills and knowledge. The activities focus on the subject content of instruction by reflecting on current content being taught and identifying gaps in content. Finally, the DEC model has a sustained approach by planning with improvement teams to establish school-level workshops and technical assistance to meet the needs identified by their own data analysis.

Content Alignment Analysis

The two-dimensional grid or content matrix of the survey instrument is used to collect data from teachers on the subject content taught in class, and the same matrix is used to analyze and quantify the subject content represented in state tests and standards. A simplified example of the grid is shown in Figure 1. The degree of consistency, or alignment, between the content reported by teachers and the subject content analyzed in state standards or assessments is reported as an alignment statistic, which can be a dependent variable measuring change in instruction, or the statistic can be an intervening measure that explains effects of instruction on achievement. The horizontal dimension represents time or emphasis on topics and the vertical dimension represents emphasis on cognitive demand. The third dimension produced from the data is the relative time or emphasis placed on topics and cognitive demand.

To produce the standards/assessments content analyses, three or more subject specialists independently judge for each standard benchmark statement or assessment item which cells in the two-dimensional grid represent the content a student is expected to know. The content specialists are trained in the SEC procedures to obtain consistency in definitions and approach. The content analysis score for a given state document is an average of responses across the team.

Software to Analyze Instructional Data and Produce Graphics

The detailed instructional data produced from teacher surveys using the SEC content matrix, with an average of 350 cells, and the data from the expert teams' analysis of content of standards (using the same matrix) are converted into proportions of emphasis for each cell such that the marginal proportions sum to 1. The data are presented in a graphic form using either a topographical mapping program or a tile format (using Excel and Corel presentations). Figures 2.1 and 2.2 illustrate the use of a topographical map to display teacher survey data and content standards in middle grades math from one of the DEC study sites.

Collaborative Improvement Strategies with Schools Using Data

The DEC model is based on several areas of research and development on instructional improvement strategies with teachers. The work of Schmoker (2001) and Fullan (2002) on effective strategies for improving student achievement was used to inform the group training process with teams and then teachers. The processes for working with educators through hands-on activities, school leader teams, simulations, and direct engagement with instructional and curriculum data have been adapted from Love (2001) and Garmston and Wellman (1999). Further guidance for the DEC professional development design has come from the work of Loucks-Horsley et al. (1998) on effective professional development in science and math and the important leading studies of professional development strategies of Cohen and Hill (2001) and Garet et al. (2001).

Finally, we drew from the work of several scholars on data-based decision making for raising student achievement (Creighton 2001; Smith and Freeman 2002; Streifer 2001; Yeagley 2001) and the growing literature on using data from classroom and large-scale assessments to guide instrument improvement (Wiggins and McTighe 1998; Guskey 2003; Commission on Instructionally Supportive Assessment 2001; Gandal and McGiffert 2003).

Longitudinal Study Design with Urban Middle Schools

The study design to test the DEC instructional improvement model consisted of place-based randomized trials, with middle schools in large urban districts randomly assigned to the treatment or control condition. The sample consisted of 50 middle schools located in five urban districts: Charlotte-Mecklenburg, Chicago, Miami-

Categories of Cognitive Demand					
Math Content Topics	Memorize	Perform Procedures	Communicate Understanding	Solve Non-Routine Problems	Conjecture, Generalize, Prove
Number Sense/ Properties/ Relationships					
Measurement					
Data Analysis/ Probability/ Statistics					
Algebraic Concepts					
Geometric Concepts					
Instructional Technology					

Dade, Philadelphia, and Winston-Salem. The study team collected baseline survey data using group administration in spring 2001. Surveys were completed by 604 middle grades math and science teachers, representing just over 75 percent of all math and science teachers in those schools. Seventy percent of the teachers were female, 40 percent White, 33 percent African American, and 20 percent Hispanic. The majority of teachers were generalists, with just 9 percent having mathematics education as their major and 6 percent with science education as their major. Twenty-seven percent of the teachers reported they had received more than 100 hours of professional development in the preceding two years. Twenty-three percent reported having received less than 30 hours, and 8 percent reported having received no professional development in the preceding two years (Porter et al. 2005).

The independent variable—the DEC instructional improvement model—introduced from 2001 to 2003 was the treatment condition (provided in half the randomly selected schools) versus the control condition (model not provided in the other half of schools). The control condition could not be absolute. The control schoolteachers continued to participate in other professional development, and the teachers in the treatment schools participated in professional development other than the DEC model. The study, however, did examine these differences by collecting data not only

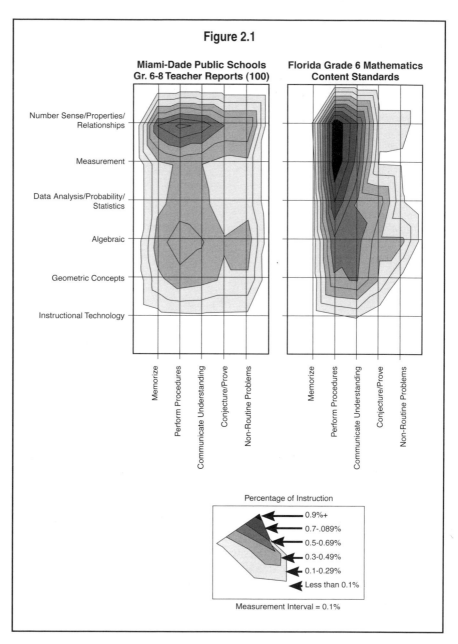

Figure 2.1

on the quality of the treatment implementation, but also on the other professional development experiences of both the treatment and control schoolteachers.

The treatment does not prescribe what is to happen in each participating teacher's classroom. Rather, it specifies professional development in which leadership teams initially participate and receive training on data-driven improvement strategies.

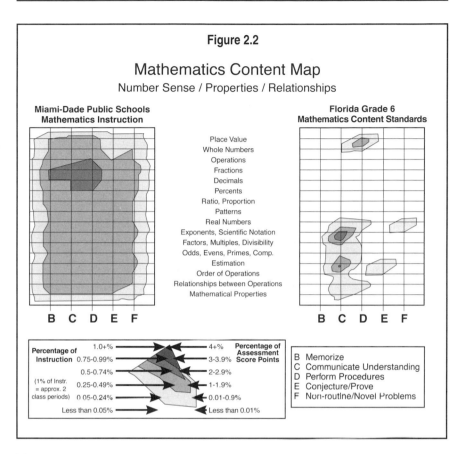

Figure 2.2

Mathematics Content Map
Number Sense / Properties / Relationships

Miami-Dade Public Schools Mathematics Instruction

Florida Grade 6 Mathematics Content Standards

Place Value
Whole Numbers
Operations
Fractions
Decimals
Percents
Ratio, Proportion
Patterns
Real Numbers
Exponents, Scientific Notation
Factors, Multiples, Divisibility
Odds, Evens, Primes, Comp.
Estimation
Order of Operations
Relationships between Operations
Mathematical Properties

B   C   D   E   F   B   C   D   E   F

Percentage of Instruction		Percentage of Assessment Score Points
1.0+%		4+%
0.75-0.99%		3-3.9%
0.5-0.74%		2-2.9%
0.25-0.49%		1-1.9%
0.05-0.24%		0.01-0.9%
Less than 0.05%		Less than 0.01%

(1% of Instr. = approx. 2 class periods)

B Memorize
C Communicate Understanding
D Perform Procedures
E Conjecture/Prove
F Non-routine/Novel Problems

The team members, in turn, provide professional development to their colleagues in their schools. The professional development is aimed at helping teachers reflect on their individual and collective practices, and from that reflection they are to decide how their instruction might be strengthened, such as by changing or decreasing variation in practices across classrooms or by providing intensive subject preparation for teachers.

After two years of the treatment versus control condition, the research team collected 439 follow-up teacher surveys in the same set of schools surveyed in study year 1. Several schools had dropped out of the study due to leadership change and district political issues, and many teachers had moved out of the study schools (Blank et al. 2004) and as a result, longitudinal survey data were obtained from 72 percent of the initial sample of teachers.

A key dependent variable in the study is the degree of change in alignment between the content of each teacher's instruction and the content of the state standards and state- or districtwide assessments used for accountability purposes. We hypothesized that the greater the effect of the treatment, the greater the alignment of teachers' content practices with the standards and assessments used with their students. Each treatment school selected a specific focus target of improvement based on analysis of their baseline data and the target was related to a content area or learning expectations, and these target standards served as a dependent variable measuring the effects of the DEC model.

Measuring Effects of the Model on Instruction

This study reports the effects of the DEC model using summary statistics of the amount of change and significance of differences from year 1 (2001 baseline) to year 3 (2003 follow-up survey). A paper describing analysis of the DEC model treatment effects has been published by Porter et al. (2006). In the present paper, we highlight some of the key findings for educators and decision makers who are interested in replicating or adapting the model. Figure 3 shows the change in alignment between instruction and target standards for the math teachers and the science teachers. These results show that across the whole sample of teachers—math and science, including treatment and control groups—instruction increased in consistency with standards. On a scale of 0 to 1, science instructional alignment increased from .18 to .20, while math instruction increased from .32 to .36 (both significant changes). This finding likely shows that standards-focused change of various kinds in these districts was having some impact on teaching in math and science.

Figure 4 highlights the degree of improvement in alignment of instruction in three teacher groups—treatment, leader, and control. The change results in Figure 4 clearly

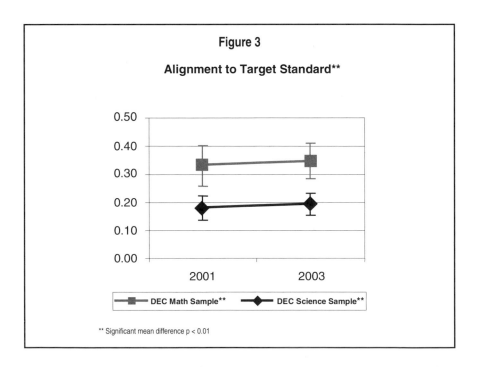

Figure 3

Alignment to Target Standard**

** Significant mean difference p < 0.01

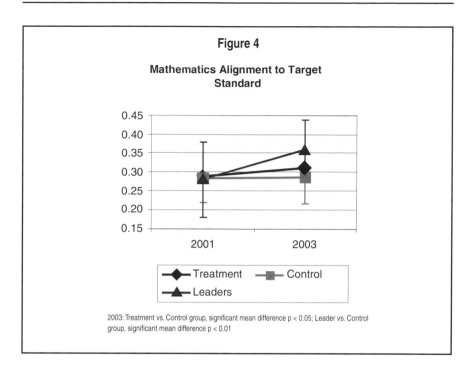

Figure 4

Mathematics Alignment to Target Standard

2003: Treatment vs. Control group, significant mean difference p < 0.05; Leader vs. Control group, significant mean difference p < 0.01

show positive effects of the DEC model. First, math teachers in the treatment schools gained in alignment of instruction to target math standards compared with teachers in control schools (in year 3, treatment group alignment = .31 versus control = .29). This shows the DEC model had effects on improving mathematics instruction for teachers in treatment schools compared with teachers in schools that did not experience the DEC professional development.

Another key finding is that the math teachers serving on leader teams in the treatment schools had a significantly greater gain in alignment of instruction than either group (i.e., change in alignment of instruction from year 1 to year 3). The analysis of the treatment effects data by Porter et al. (2006) showed the effect size of the change in instructional alignment for the leader group of teachers is equal to .36 (or 36 percent gain), which represents a moderate but certainly meaningful level of change. The finding is significant in relation to the DEC model because these teachers received the most intensive and consistent training in analysis and use of data to identify ways to improve instruction. We did not, however, find a comparable level of change in instructional alignment of leader teachers in science. One explanation is that most schools chose focused targets for improvement related to math content.

Measures of Model Implementation

Our analysis of variables that may have produced DEC model results included measures of change in teacher preparation, school conditions, and professional develop-

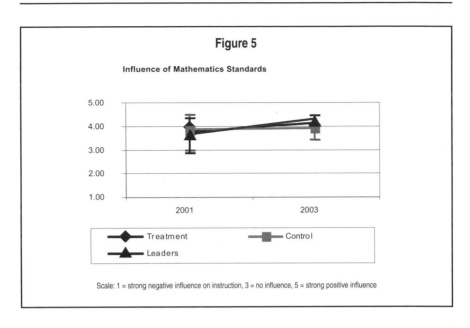

Figure 5

Influence of Mathematics Standards

Scale: 1 = strong negative influence on instruction, 3 = no influence, 5 = strong positive influence

ment activities. We highlight three measures of professional development as reported by teachers in the study that help explain the effects of the DEC model. Figure 5 displays change in teachers' reporting on what influences their instruction, specifically the degree to which state content standards affect what they teach. In year 1, there was significant variation in influence of standards, but all three groups averaged between 3 and 4 (none to positive). In year 3 after the DEC treatment, however, the math leader teachers reported significant increases in the influence of math standards on their instruction, with average after two years above 4 (positive influence).

A second measure of DEC model implementation is change in indicators of the quality of professional development activities reported by sample teachers. The teachers were asked to report on the presence and/or absence of a range of activity types, including college content courses, inservice workshops, and within-school work with colleagues and professional practice networks. (See SEC survey instrument for full listing of the items on professional development activities at http://www.SECsurvey. org.) Survey item responses were analyzed using four scales of quality of professional development received by teachers. These items and scales are designed to analyze the range of professional development activities and opportunities received by teachers during the prior 12 months; thus, they include the activities as part of the DEC treatment as well as other forms of professional development received by teachers.

The analysis of change in professional development quality scales from year 1 to year 3 of the study showed significant improvement in quality reported by mathematics teachers. (See figure 6.) The four scales are based on the results of research on characteristics of effective professional development (e.g., Garet et al. 2001). The scales vary from 0 to 1, with 1 meaning all professional development quality items

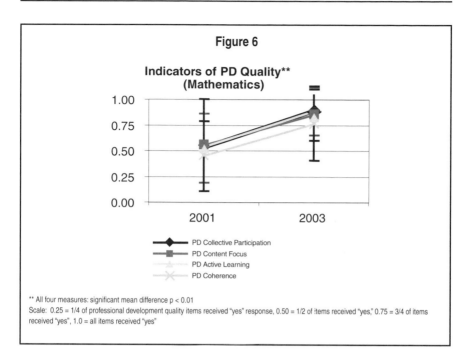

Figure 6

Indicators of PD Quality**
(Mathematics)

Legend:
- PD Collective Participation
- PD Content Focus
- PD Active Learning
- PD Coherence

** All four measures: significant mean difference p < 0.01

Scale: 0.25 = 1/4 of professional development quality items received "yes" response, 0.50 = 1/2 of items received "yes," 0.75 = 3/4 of items received "yes", 1.0 = all items received "yes"

received a "yes" response. In year 1, all four scales (collective participation, content focus, active learning, coherence) were very close to .5—which means half of the teachers' professional development experiences were not consistent with quality measures. After the introduction and experience with the DEC treatment model, in year 3, the same teachers reported an average quality of all professional development in four scales above .75, which represents a 50 percent increase in reported quality of professional development received by math teachers. Also noteworthy is the significant decrease in the extent of variation in responses (indicated by the whisker plots for 1 standard deviation above/below the means).

A third measure of effects of the DEC model is change in time and effort of teachers on professional development. Figure 7 data show the average time span of professional development activities reported by math teachers in 2001 (study year 1) compared with 2003 (study year 3). For both treatment and control groups, the average time span in year 1 was a single workshop, and within one standard deviation a significant portion of teachers experienced a single workshop with follow-up activities. In year 3 of the study, the average math teachers in both treatment and control groups received a single workshop with follow-up, and a significant portion of teachers experienced multiple workshops.

Summary of Findings from Longitudinal Analysis

Our review of findings from the DEC experimental design study have focused on several of the significant results regarding change over time for schools and teachers

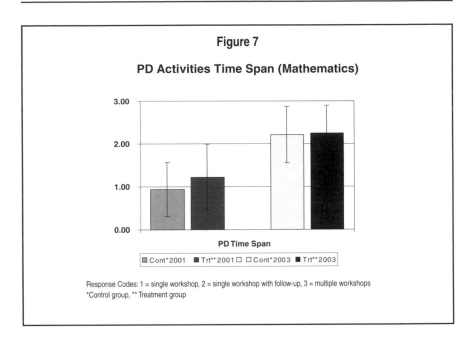

Figure 7

PD Activities Time Span (Mathematics)

Response Codes: 1 = single workshop, 2 = single workshop with follow-up, 3 = multiple workshops
*Control group, ** Treatment group

in the treatment group compared with those in the control group. A basic pattern across all the schools in the study (treatment and control) is greater alignment of instruction with standards from inception to year 3. This pattern held in both math and science. In mathematics, the analysis showed group teachers, and especially leader team members, had significantly greater improvement in aligned instruction than the control group, indicating the DEC model's approach to instructional improvement was effective in math, but showed less effects in science. It should be noted that improvement of instruction was measured in relation to the specific standards selected by schools.

Finally, the longitudinal findings show change in the types of professional activities, shifting from single workshops to multiple session activities, and mathematics teachers reported significantly greater quality of professional development activities at the end of the DEC treatment compared with the baseline data on their professional development.

How the DEC Model Works

The basic findings outlined from the three-year longitudinal study provide support for the premise that the DEC model for instructional improvement can have positive effects in many schools and districts. More detailed analysis and description of study findings have been provided in other papers (Porter 2002; Blank et al. 2004). But, how does the model actually work? How do the professional development activities through the implemented DEC model work to influence change in teaching practices? What are the key steps in the model for educating teachers?

The DEC professional development model for improving instruction is based on three primary goals:

1. focus on developing skills of educators and continuous improvement of classroom practices using data and formative evaluation;

2. standards-based improvement of instruction and use of data on alignment with standards to identify weaknesses and gaps in instruction; and

3. school-based collaboration, technical assistance, and networking among teachers to foster the sharing of teaching ideas, models, and strategies for improvement.

The five large urban districts that volunteered to participate in the study were similar in expressing commitment to standards-based improvement of math and science, and support for the concepts in the DEC model. The DEC treatment schools were asked to form a five- to seven-member mathematics and science school leader team at the outset of the project. The teams included at least one administrator—the principal or the assistant principal for curriculum—mathematics and science department chairs, lead or master mathematics and science teachers, and other math and science teachers such that a range of grades and subjects were represented. The teams participated in all project professional development workshops and meetings throughout the treatment. For further details on the DEC model organization and activities, see Nunnaley (2003).

In addition to the school leadership teams, the DEC treatment calls for each district contact person to involve district-level instructional specialists by inviting them to participate in all the workshops. Districts have the option of scheduling separate workshops for entire district groups in supporting mathematics and science instruction in the schools. The rationale for involving a larger support network is to ensure everyone working in the schools has knowledge of the processes, techniques, and goals of the DEC work.

Developing Knowledge and Skills of Educators in Using Data

The DEC professional development model recognizes that few teachers, or administrators, have previously been involved in a professional development process to teach them how to analyze and use data on curriculum or student achievement. The DEC trainer staff introduces to school leader teams the skills for leading collaborative work with a group of professionals, how to provide training on data analysis, and how to ask tough questions about which students are/are not learning, what content is being learned, and why some students are not learning. The leader team workshops model best practices in data analysis and in teaching specific subject-area topics, and provide support and strategies for how to engage colleagues.

Table 1—Schedule for DEC Professional Development (PD) Model

Year 1:	Spring	Orientation of district and school leaders; teachers complete baseline SEC
	Summer-Early Fall	Introductory PD workshop for leader teams (two days); develop data skills and begin data inquiry training
	Late Fall	Technical assistance in schools to introduce model to teachers (leader half-day session each school)
Year 2:	Winter	PD workshop #2: Use of content data and instructional practices data (one to two days)
	Spring Year 2	Technical assistance in schools to set school targets for improvement based on data analysis; integrate model with other PD in subject area
	Spring	PD workshop #3: Analyzing student work and comparing instructional strategies (one day)
	Summer to Fall	Technical assistance in school teams; work with teachers to apply data to instruction; identify additional PD needs
	Fall Year 2	Evaluate progress toward improvement objectives; re-focus efforts within schools; continue team interaction
Year 3:	Winter	Teachers continue work in teams and apply data lessons to improved teaching strategies; continue team interaction
	Spring Year 3	Complete follow-up surveys with teachers to assess change at end of second year of PD model

District and School Responsibilities

Table 1 provides a summary outline of the schedule and scope of main activities in the DEC professional development model as it was presented to the participating districts. In year 1 at the orientation stage of the DEC model, the CCSSO team outlined the key responsibilities of the districts and schools for effective implementation:

- regularly scheduled meeting times for school leadership teams and time commitment for teachers to work on applying the model;

- decision-making support for next steps in schools;

- inclusion of the DEC model in school and district professional development;

- access to school data including state assessment results; and

- focus on measurable results.

After the orientation, each school selected and organized a school leader team for implementing the DEC model. Initial workshop training was geared toward the leadership teams and focused on developing data skills and inquiry approaches with data. The training provided leaders with a design and sequence of activities for working with teachers to bring the model into schools. (For a full explanation and detail on the DEC model design, see Nunnaley 2003.) School leader teams were provided skills in leading workshops with teachers. In addition, school teams identified ways to integrate the DEC model for using curriculum data with other professional development activities and strategies within the school. It is critical for teams to develop a coherent approach to subject-area professional development and instructional improvement with the school. Leader teams also work to develop a long-term plan for using the data-driven model with teachers.

Standards-Based Improvement of Instruction Using Analysis of Alignment

The DEC model is grounded with research-based tools (Surveys of Enacted Curriculum) that provide the capacity for describing instructional practices at the school level (both pedagogy and content) based on responses from all teachers of a given subject and grade, as well as tools for describing the content of the intended curriculum (e.g., expressed in content standards and assessments) through measures of the nature and degree of alignment between instructional practices and curriculum materials (Porter 2002). The treatment model can be understood in part by the nature of the data provided to school leadership teams and other teachers in the treatment schools.

All teachers in a target school report on their instructional subject content and teaching practices for the prior school year. The content of instruction is reported using a two-dimensional grid. (See the two dimensions—content by expectations—in Figure 1; for complete survey instrument and grid, see http://www.SEConline.org.) Data reporting entails three steps:

1. The teacher works through the list of specific topics (e.g., for math: number sense, operations, measurement, algebraic concepts, geometric concepts, etc.), reporting on which of the topics were taught.

2. For the specific topics taught, the teacher describes degree of content coverage on a five-point scale for each specific subtopic (e.g., for numbers: place value, whole numbers, fractions, ratio, etc.), indicating whether the coverage represented (a) less than one class/lesson, (b) one to five classes/lessons, or (c) more than five classes/lessons.

3. For each subtopic covered, the teacher indicates which of the five categories of cognitive demand were taught (i.e., memorize, perform procedures, demonstrate understanding, prove, make connections), and for those that were taught, the degree of emphasis. The three-point emphasis scale distinguishes (a) slight emphasis (less than 25 percent of the time spent on the topic), (b) moderate emphasis (25-33 percent of the time spent on the topic), and (c) sustained emphasis (more than 33 percent of the time spent on the topic).

With the complete data report for each teacher's course/class, a content map is constructed showing the proportion of emphasis on topics by expectations/cognitive demand. Then, data are aggregated by school, and content maps can be compared across schools and classrooms. The first major step in technical assistance is to produce content maps for each school with data disaggregated by grade and class characteristics (e.g., achievement level or percentage of limited English speakers).

State standards and assessments are content coded by expert subject specialists using the same SEC content matrix (often in multi-state workshops). With the coding results, schools and teachers can compare their instruction with the standards defined by the state, both by topic and by expectations for learning. One type of "alignment analysis" used in schools involves visual comparison of content of instruction, which does not require statistical analysis or interpretation. But, the alignment data analysis does produce a statistic of degree of alignment, or "alignment index," which varies from 0 (no consistency) to 1 (perfect consistency) (Porter and Smithson 2002). For example, in the DEC study (Figure 2.1), the alignment index for Miami grade 6 math instruction (treatment schools) with Florida state standards was 0.19. (See Porter and Smithson [2001] for further explanation of alignment analysis procedures.)

School-Based Collaboration among Educators

Professional development for all educators with the DEC model begins with training in data skills, including how to analyze and apply the enacted curriculum data charts and how to interpret differences in the contour maps and bar graphs signifying high and low emphases of instruction across a school or district. The school team gains skills in the collaborative analysis method starting with one data chart (e.g., one subject topic area). Educators analyze their own school instructional data building from their experience of completing the survey, their knowledge of instruction in the school, and their team interaction about data variation they observe and discussion about sources of differences in instruction.

Three-Step Process

DEC leader teams work with teachers by subject area through a three-step process—predict, observe/analyze, and interpret. Teachers are asked first to predict what they will see in the degree of consistency, or alignment, between math instruction and district and state standards (e.g., Florida middle math standards). In step two, educators look at the charts for math instruction and standards for their district and state. Educators work together in teams to share what they see—which topics and expectations have high emphases of time and how consistent they are with the standards. For example, Figures 2.1 and 2.2 show data from Miami study schools by middle grades math content area. Miami math educators could see instruction in grades 6 through 8 strongly emphasized number sense, while the Florida standards emphasized number sense, measurement, and data analysis for grade 6 instruction.

In step three, educators refer to a chart that analyzes the content of instruction in their school, with charts such as those in Figure 2.2 reported by school. Data results can be compared from school to school, and then with state standards. Teachers compare and contrast instructional content (topic by expectations) in their classroom and school with other classrooms and across schools in their district, and teachers also can compare their instructional differences with classroom and school assessment results by topic area. Teachers can obtain a chart of their own instructional content and compare it with the average instruction for teachers in the school. Thus, teachers identify the differences between their instruction and instruction of others in their schools as well as in the overall district. Teachers engage in discussions about the differences in instruction they observe, how and why differences in instruction develop, and what effects these differences may mean for students.

Drill Down by Topic

Another approach to using the data is to "drill down" to look at instruction on specific topics in the curriculum. For example, the Miami middle grades math instruction map shown in Figure 2.1 can be broken out for each content topic (number sense, measurement, algebra, etc.), and Figure 2.2 shows such a map for the number sense topic. Then, in analyzing instruction in middle grades math, the topic of number sense, for example, which typically receives a high degree of emphasis in the early elementary grades, can be analyzed in more detail to see what subtopics under number sense should (or should not) be receiving instructional time at middle grades. Critiques of the U.S. math curriculum focus on excessive repetition of topics across the grades, and the instructional maps allow schools to address appropriate versus excessive repetition of content topics. Subtopics are useful for educator team analysis because they likely correspond to the organization of the teacher's lesson plans and course outlines. The analysis showed Miami teachers emphasized numbers related to operations in all three of the middle grades, while the Florida standards placed emphasis on patterns, exponents, factors, and estimation.

Analysis and Technical Assistance Process in Schools

The evidence from the DEC longitudinal study shows that when school teams fully implement the model, the data analysis process becomes an important lever for change. A key role of leader teams, including administrators, is scheduling regular training and technical assistance sessions to ensure follow-up, continued data analyses within schools, and increased depth of analysis. Teachers share ideas and strategies for focusing their instructional strategies and practices to increase alignment. Leaders have a key role in identifying needs, based on school-level analysis, for further content-specific professional development that may need to be provided from specialists. The goal is to build a professional learning community based on continued, ongoing use of data to identify learning gaps and issues, focus improvement efforts, evaluate progress, and then repeat the process of data use.

References

Black, P., & Wiliam, D. (1998). Assessment and classroom learning. *Assessment in Education, 5*(1), 7-74.

Blank, R.K., Nunnaley, D., Kaufman, M., Porter, A.C., Smithson, J., Osthoff, E., et al. (2004). *Data on enacted curriculum study: Summary of findings. Experimental design study of effectiveness of DEC professional development model in urban middle schools.* Washington, DC: Council of Chief State School Officers. Retrieved April 29, 2005, from http://www.ccsso.org/content/pdfs/DECStudy.pdf

Blank, R.K., Porter, A.C., & Smithson, J. (2001). *New tools for analyzing teaching, curriculum and standards: Results from the surveys of enacted curriculum project.* Washington, DC: Council of Chief State School Officers.

Borman, G.D., Hewes, G.M., Overman, L.T., & Brown, S. (2002). *Comprehensive school reform and student achievement: A meta-analysis.* Baltimore, MD: Center for Research on the Education of Students Placed at Risk.

Cohen, D.K., & Hill, H.C. (2001). *Learning policy: When state education reform works.* New Haven, CT: Yale University Press.

Commission on Instructionally Supportive Assessment. (2001). *Building tests that support instruction and accountability: A guide for policymakers.* Washington, DC: Author. Retrieved May 30, 2006, from http://www.testaccountability.org/

Council of Chief State School Officers. (2002). *Experimental design to measure effects of assisting teachers in using data on enacted curriculum to improve effectiveness of instruction in mathematics and science education: Year 2 progress report.* Washington, DC: Author.

Council of Chief State School Officers. (2003). *Surveys of enacted curriculum: Surveys of classroom practices and instructional content in mathematics, science, & English language arts.* Surveys developed by CCSSO with Wisconsin Center for Education Research, SEC Collaborative, and Learning Point Associates. Washington, DC: Author. Retrieved from http://www.SECsurvey.org

Council of Chief State School Officers, & Appalachian Educational Laboratory. (2001). *Data-based decision making: Resources for educators.* Washington, DC: Author. [Online Tool]. Retrieved from http://www.ael.org/dbdm/

Creighton, T.B. (2001, May/June). Data analysis and the principalship. *Principal Leadership, 1*(9), 52-57.

Cross, C.T. (Ed.). (2004). *Putting the pieces together: Lessons from comprehensive school reform research.* Washington, DC: National Clearinghouse for Comprehensive School Reform. Retrieved May 18, 2006, from http://www.centerforcsri.org/PDF/PTPTLessonsfrom CSRResearch.pdf

Desimone, L. (2002, Fall). How can comprehensive school reform models be successfully implemented? *Review of Educational Research, 72*(3), 433-479.

Desimone, L.M., Porter, A.C., Garet, M.S., Yoon, K.S., & Birman, B.F. (2002). Effects of professional development on teachers' instruction: Results from a three-year longitudinal study. *Educational Evaluation and Policy Analysis, 24*(2), 81-112.

Edmonds, R. (1979, October). Effective schools for the urban poor. *Educational Leadership, 37*, 15-24.

Elmore, R. (2002). *Bridging the gap between standards and achievement: Report on the imperative for professional development in education.* Washington, DC: The Albert Shanker Institute. Retrieved May 30, 2005, from http://www.shankerinstitute.org/Downloads/Bridging_Gap.pdf

Fullan, M. (2002, May). The change leader. *Educational Leadership, 59*(8), 16-20.

Gamoran, A., Porter, A.C., Smithson, J., & White, P.A. (1997, Winter). Upgrading high school mathematics instruction: Improving learning opportunities for low-achieving, low-income youth. *Educational Evaluation and Policy Analysis, 19*(4), 325-338.

Gandal, M., & McGiffert, L. (2003, February). The power of testing. *Educational Leadership, 60*(5), 39-42.

Garet, M.S., Porter, A.C., Desimone, L., Birman, B.F., & Yoon, K.S. (2001). What makes professional development effective? Results from a national sample of teachers. *American Educational Research Journal, 38*(4), 915-945.

Garmston, R., & Wellman, B. (1999). *The adaptive school: A sourcebook for developing collaborative groups.* Norwood, MA: Christopher-Gordon Publishers, Inc.

Guskey, T.R. (2003, February). How classroom assessments improve learning. *Educational Leadership, 60*(5), 6-12.

Kennedy, M.M. (1998, April). *Form and substance in inservice teacher education.* Paper presented at the annual meeting of the American Educational Research Association, San Diego, CA.

Lewis, C., Perry, R., & Murata, A. (2006). How should research contribute to instructional improvement? The case of lesson study. *Educational Researcher, 35*(3), 3-14.

Loucks-Horsley, S., Hewson, P., Love, N., & Stiles, K.E. (1998). *Designing professional development for teachers of science and mathematics.* Thousand Oaks, CA: Corwin Press, Inc.

Love, N. (2001). *Using data-getting results: A practical guide to school improvement in mathematics and science.* Norwood, MA: Christopher-Gordon Publishers, Inc.

Marzano, R.J. (2003). *What works in schools: Translating research into action.* Alexandria, VA: Association for Supervision and Curriculum Development.

Nunnaley, D. (2003). *Using data on enacted curriculum.* Cambridge, MA: TERC. [PowerPoint presentation]. Retrieved May 30, 2006, from http://www.ccsso.org/content/pdfs/DianaNunalUseofSEC-Nov25.ppt

Porter, A.C. (2002). Measuring the content of instruction: Uses in research and practice. *Educational Researcher, 31*(7), 3-14.

Porter, A.C., Blank, R.K., Smithson, J., & Osthoff, E. (2005, May). Place-based randomized trials to test the effects on instructional practices of a mathematics/science professional development program for teachers. *The Annals of the American Academy of Political and Social Science, 599*(1), 147-175.

Porter, A.C., Kirst, M.W., Osthoff, E.J., Smithson, J.L., & Schneider, S.A. (1993). *Reform up close: An analysis of high school mathematics and science classrooms.* (Final report to the National Science Foundation). Madison, WI: Wisconsin Center for Education Research.

Porter, A.C., & Smithson, J. (2001). Are content standards being implemented in the classroom? A methodology and some tentative answers. In S.H. Fuhrman (Ed.), *From the capitol to the classroom: Standards-based reform in the states* (pp. 60-80). Chicago: National Society for the Study of Education.

Porter, A.C., & Smithson, J. (2002). Alignment of assessments, standards, and instruction using curriculum indicator data. Presentation at the National Council on Measurement in Education annual meeting, New Orleans, LA.

Porter, A.C., Smithson, J.L., Blank, R., & Zeidner, T. (2006, December). Alignment as a teacher variable. *Applied Measurement in Education, 20*(1) (forthcoming).

Schmoker, M. (2001). *The results field-book: Practical strategies from dramatically improved schools.* Alexandria, VA: Association for Supervision and Curriculum Development.

Schmoker, M. (2002, Spring). Up and away. *Journal of Staff Development Council, 23*(2), 12-13.

Smith, C.L., & Freeman, R.L. (2002, Summer). Using continuous system level assessment to build school capacity. *American Journal of Evaluation, 23*(3), 317-319.

Stigler, J.W., & Hiebert, J. (1997). Understanding and improving classroom mathematics instruction: An overview of the TIMSS video study. *Phi Delta Kappan, 79*(1), 14-21.

Streifer, P.A. (2001, April). The "drill down" process. *School Administrator, 58*(4), 16-19

Tushnet, N.C., Flaherty, J., & Smith, A. (2004). *Longitudinal assessment of comprehensive school reform program implementation and outcomes: First-year report.* Washington, DC: U.S. Department of Education, Policy and Program Studies Service. Retrieved May 18, 2006, from http://www.ed.gov/rschstat/eval/other/lacio/lacio-final.pdf

Weiss, I.R., Arnold, E.E., Banilower, E.R., & Soar, E.H. (2000). *Local systemic change through teacher enhancement: Year five cross-site report.* Chapel Hill, NC: Horizon Research, Inc.

Wiggins, G., & McTighe, J. (1998). *Understanding by design.* Alexandria, VA: Association for Supervision and Curriculum Development.

Yeagley, R. (2001, April). Data in your hands. *School Administrator, 58*(4), 12-15.

Rolf K. Blank is director of education indicators at the Council of Chief State School Officers in Washington, D.C.; John Smithson is director of the Measures of Enacted Curriculum project, Wisconsin Center for Education Research, University of Wisconsin-Madison, in Madison, Wis.; Andrew Porter is director of the Learning Sciences Institute and professor of Public Policy and Education at Vanderbilt University in Nashville, Tenn.; Diana Nunnaley is director of implementation and professional development of the Using Data project, TERC, in Cambridge, Mass.; and Eric Osthoff is an associate researcher, Wisconsin Center for Education Research, University of Wisconsin-Madison, in Madison, Wis.

Chapter 5: Questions for Reflection and Discussion

1. The authors cite several common themes or components in the literature on schoolwide models for instructional improvement and in the designs for Comprehensive School Reform:

   - Schoolwide improvement design involving leadership and most or all instructional staff
   - Ongoing process for instructional improvement involving administrators and teachers and including scheduled work sessions for staff and time for teacher development of content knowledge and subject-specific pedagogy
   - Structured training for staff in analyzing data on student performance and the educational environment
   - Use of disaggregated data to identify learning problems and performance gaps, with frequent use of data as a formative evaluation tool to guide instructional decisions and planning

   Review each of these components and consider to what extent they are implemented in your own school. How could each component be more effectively implemented in your own environment?

2. The DEC (Data Enacted Curriculum) model emphasizes the collection of critical indicators of instructional practices and content for a year's curriculum and use of Web-based surveys to analyze instruction across many teachers, schools, and districts. What do you see as the barriers to implementation of such an approach in your own school and district?

3. Examine the feasibility of implementing the DEC professional development model in your school district. What barriers to implementation to you foresee, and how could they be addressed?

4. Consider the role of the leader teams in the DEC model. How well equipped do you think you are for this role? How about the other leaders in your school?

Section Two:

Leading By Example: Principals and Managerial Leadership

6 Developing the Science of Educational Leadership

Tim Waters, Robert J. Marzano, and Brian McNulty

Researchers from Mid-continent Research for Education and Learning (McREL) have analyzed thousands of quantitative studies published over the last 30 years to determine what works in classrooms and in schools. In two earlier meta-analyses, McREL identified teacher and school practices that have the largest effects on student achievement.

McREL has completed a third meta-analysis of the effects of school leadership on student achievement. The authors assert the strength of this relationship and provide straightforward and compelling guidance to superintendents, principals, and others responsible for improving school performance.

Nearly 30 years ago, the pioneers of "effective schools" research found certain school, classroom, and leadership practices are critical to enhanced student achievement and school productivity. In their initial studies, researchers such as Edmonds (1979), Brookover and Lezotte (1979), Weber (1971), and Glenn (1981) reported on the "correlates" of effective schools: high expectations for student learning, monitoring of student progress, a safe and orderly climate, an emphasis on basic skill acquisition, and strong instructional leadership. They argued improving practices consistent with these correlates was likely to result in improved student test scores. Building on these early efforts, numerous researchers have contributed to the body of knowledge known as effective schools research, adding breadth and depth to the knowledge base available to practitioners committed to improving these practices.

Since 1998, McREL researchers have been engaged in what might be referred to as "third generation" effective schools research, distinguishing it from the efforts in the 1980s to implement the research findings from the 1970s. The organization has synthesized hundreds of studies completed since the early 1970s, through a series of meta-analyses of research on the student characteristics, school practices, and teacher practices associated with student achievement.

The first analysis in this series, *A Theory-Based Meta-Analysis of Research on Instruction* (Marzano, 1998), which included more than 110 reports, examined the effects of a variety of classroom instructional strategies on achievement. (This study can be found on McREL's Web site at www.mcrel.org.) It organized this research into nine clusters of instructional strategies that, if used skillfully, have a high probability of enhancing classroom instruction and, concomitantly, student academic achievement. This report, now published as the book *Classroom Instruction that Works* (Marzano, Pickering, & Pollock, 2001), provides teachers with guidance on using the nine categories of instructional strategies highly correlated with high levels of student achievement.

The second meta-analysis, which included more than 150 research reports, was published by McREL as *A New Era of School Reform* (Marzano, 2000). (This report also can be found on McREL's Website.) In this study, the author reported on school and classroom practices that account for substantial variances in student achievement between effective and ineffective schools.

McREL's third meta-analysis has focused on the effects of principal leadership on student achievement. This study involved review of more than 5,000 studies—published since the early 1970s—purported to have examined the effects of leadership. From these 5,000 studies, 70 met the following criteria for design, controls, data analysis, and rigor:

- quantitative student achievement data;

- student achievement measured on standardized, norm-referenced tests or some other objective measure of achievement;

- student achievement as the dependent variable; and

- teacher perceptions of leadership as the independent variable.

These 70 studies involved 2,894 schools, approximately 1.1 million students, and 14,000 teachers. To our knowledge, this represents the largest sample of principals, teachers, and student achievement scores ever used to analyze the effects of educational leadership. In the aggregate, these findings provide straightforward and compelling guidance for policy makers, superintendents, principals, aspiring principals, school leadership teams, and those involved in administrator preparation.

Findings

Three major findings from our initial analysis are of immediate use to educational leaders. The first is that we can now quantify the general effect of leadership. We have known since the early days of effective schools research that instructional leadership is correlated with student achievement. We can now reasonably assert the strength of the correlation: .25. We provide an explanation of this finding in the following section of this article.

Our second finding adds specificity and detail to the first. We have identified 66 leadership practices embedded in 21 leadership responsibilities, each with statistically significant relationships to student achievement. Each of these responsibilities is described in greater detail later in Figure 3.

Our third finding is that teacher perceptions of principal leadership, while significantly correlated to higher levels of student achievement, can be negatively correlated to achievement. We have labeled this as the "differential impact" of leadership, as explained later in this article.

The General Effect of Leadership

As stated earlier, the first finding of this study is the strength of the correlation between principal leadership and student achievement. We found the average effect size (expressed as a correlation) between leadership and student achievement is .25. A graphic depiction of the correlation is presented in Figures 1 and 2.

To interpret this correlation, consider two schools (school A and school B) with similar student and teacher populations. Both demonstrate achievement on a standardized, norm-referenced test at the 50th percentile. Principals in both schools are also average—that is, their abilities in the 21 key leadership responsibilities are ranked at the 50th percentile. Now assume the principal of school B improves her demonstrated abilities in all 21 responsibilities by exactly one standard deviation. (See Figure 1.)

The research findings indicate this increase in leadership ability would translate into an expected mean student achievement at school B that is 10 percentile points higher than school A, as depicted in figure 2. Expressed differently, a one standard deviation improvement in leadership practices is associated with an increase in average student achievement from the 50th percentile to the 60th percentile.

Principal Leadership Responsibilities

In addition to finding a general correlation between effective leadership and student achievement, we were able to more clearly define effective leadership as 66 practices grouped into 21 leadership responsibilities that are positively correlated with student achievement. These responsibilities and the practices associated with them are shown in figure 3. It is important to note that each of the correlations (r) reported in figure 3 is statistically significant.

The "Differential Impact" of Leadership

The third major finding from our analysis focuses on the "differential impact" of leadership. That is, just as leaders can have a positive impact on achievement, they also can have a marginal or—even worse—a *negative* impact on achievement. When leaders concentrate on the wrong school and/or classroom practices, or miscalculate

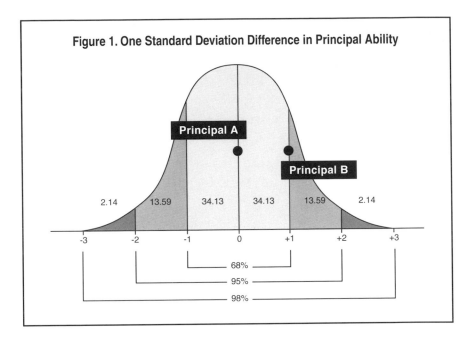

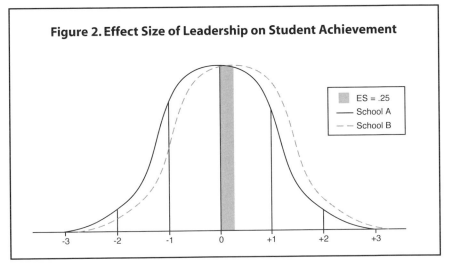

the magnitude or "order" of the change they are attempting to implement, they can have a negative impact on student achievement. Figure 4 displays the range of impact leaders can have on student performance. In some studies, we found an effect size of .50 for leadership and achievement. This means a one standard deviation difference in demonstrated leadership ability is associated with as much as a 19 percentile point increase in student achievement—an increase that is substantially larger than the 10 percentile point increase mentioned previously.

In other studies, we found correlations as low as -.02. This indicates that schools where principals demonstrated higher competence in certain leadership areas had *lower* levels of student achievement. In these studies, a one standard deviation improvement in leadership practices was correlated with a one percentile point *decrease* in student achievement.

What can we learn from this 20 percentile difference in the impact of leadership? We have concluded there are two primary variables that determine whether or not leadership will have a positive or negative impact on achievement. The first is the **focus of change**—that is, whether leaders properly identify and focus on improving the school and classroom practices most likely to have a positive impact on student achievement in their school. The second variable is whether leaders properly understand the magnitude or **"order" of change** they are leading and adjust their leadership practices accordingly. We discuss these variables in greater detail in the following sections.

The Focus of Change

Harvard scholar Richard Elmore, in a study commissioned by the National Governors Association (NGA), concluded that having the right focus of change is a key to improving schools and increasing student achievement. In his report for NGA, *Knowing the Right Thing to Do: School Improvement and Performance-Based Accountability*, he states:

> Knowing the right thing to do is the central problem of school improvement. Holding schools accountable for their performance depends on having people in schools with the knowledge, skill, and judgment to make the improvements that will increase student performance (Elmore, 2003, p. 9).

We reached the same conclusion to help explain the differential impact of leadership. Through the two meta-analyses mentioned earlier, we believe we have identified the "right things to do" to improve school effectiveness. The "right things" include the school and teacher practices listed in figure 5. For definitions and effect sizes, see McREL's report *A New Era of School Reform* (Marzano 2000), which is available for free download on McREL's Web site.

Not all principals who set out to do the right things will experience the same levels of success. In some cases, staff members may resist or sabotage these changes. In other cases, they may simply lack the requisite skills or background knowledge needed to carry out the changes. In any case, doing the right things may require an initiative to change policies, programs, practices, or procedures. If these changes have "second order" implications for teachers and other stakeholders, the principal can predict resistance, even to the best ideas motivated by the best intentions. Leaders need to understand the magnitude of the changes they are attempting to lead, the predictable reactions to first- versus second-order change, and how to tailor their leadership practices accordingly if their leadership is to have its intended effect on student achievement.

The Magnitude or "Order" of Change

The theoretical literature on leadership, change, and the adoption of new ideas—including Heifetz (1994),Fullan (1993), Beckard and Pritchard (1992), Hesselbein and Johnston (2002), Bridges (1991), Rogers (1995), Nadler, Shaw, and Walton (1994), and Kanter (1985)—makes the case that not all change is of the same magnitude. Some changes have greater implications than others for staff members, students, parents, and other stakeholders. Although there are various labels given to differing magnitudes of change (technical versus adaptive, incremental versus fundamental, continuous versus discontinuous), we have used the terms "first-order" and "second-order" change to make this distinction. Figure 6 highlights some of the differences between first- and second-order change.

It is important to note that not all changes have the same implications for each individual or stakeholder group. What will be experienced as a first-order change for some may be a second-order change for others. Assuming all change will have the same implications for all stakeholders, and/or using practices that might be appropriate for a first- order change when a second-order change is actually implied for stakeholders, will likely result in a negative impact on student achievement. Thus, in addition to focusing leadership efforts on school and classroom practices associated with improved student achievement, leaders also must tailor their own leadership practices based on the magnitude or "order" of change they are leading.

What determines the magnitude or order of change for individuals, organizations, and institutions are the implications of the change for each. On both individual and collective levels, the following changes can be considered first order:

1. They are consistent with existing values and norms.

2. They create advantages for individuals or stakeholder groups with similar interests.

3. They can be implemented with existing knowledge and resources.

4. Agreement exists on what changes are needed and on how the changes should be implemented.

In an educational context, these might be new classroom instructional practices, instructional materials, curricular programs, or data collection and reporting systems that build on established patterns and utilize existing knowledge.

A change becomes second order when:

1. It is not obvious how it will make things better for people with similar interests.

Figure 3.
Principal Leadership Responsibilities, Average r, and Leadership Practices

Responsibilities	The extent to which the principal ...	Avg r	Practices associated with responsibilities
Culture	fosters shared beliefs & a sense of community & cooperation	.29	• Promotes cooperation among staff • Promotes a sense of well-being • Promotes cohesion among staff • Develops an understanding of purpose • Develops a shared vision of what the school could be like
Order	establishes a set of standard operating procedures & routines	.26	• Provides & enforces clear structure, rules, and procedures for students • Provides & enforces clear structures, rules, and procedures for staff • Establishes routines regarding the running of the school that staff understand and follow
Discipline	protects teachers from issues & influences that would detract from their teaching time or focus	.24	• Protects instructional time from interruptions • Protects/shelters teachers from distractions
Resources	provides teachers with materials & professional development necessary for the successful execution of their jobs	.26	• Ensures teachers have necessary materials & equipment • Ensures teachers have necessary staff development opportunities that directly enhance their teaching
Curriculum, instruction, assessment	is directly involved in the design & implementation of curriculum, instruction, & assessment practices	.16	• Is involved in helping teachers design curricular activities • Is involved with teachers to address instructional issues in their classrooms • Is involved with teachers to address assessment issues
Focus	establishes clear goals & keeps those goals in the forefront of the school's attention	.24	• Establishes high, concrete goals & expectations that all students meet them • Establishes concrete goals for all curriculum, instruction, & assessment • Establishes concrete goals for the general functioning of the school • Continually keeps attention on established goals
Knowledge of curriculum, instruction, assessment	is knowledgeable about current curriculum, instruction, & assessment practices	.24	• Is knowledgeable about instructional practices • Is knowledgeable about assessment practices • Provides conceptual guidance for teachers regarding effective classroom practice

Figure 3 (continued).
Principal Leadership Responsibilities, Average r, and Leadership Practices

Responsibilities	The extent to which the principal ...	Avg r	Practices associated with responsibilities
Visibility	has quality contact & interactions with teachers & students	.16	• Makes systematic frequent visits to classrooms • Maintains high visibility around the school • Has frequent contact with students
Contingent rewards	recognizes & rewards individual accomplishments	.15	• Recognizes individuals who excel • Uses performance versus seniority as the primary criterion for reward & advancement • Uses hard work & results as the basis for reward & recognition
Communication	establishes strong lines of communication with teachers & among students	.23	• Is easily accessible to teachers • Develops effective means for teachers to communicate with one another • Maintains open and effective lines of communication with staff
Outreach	is an advocate & spokesperson for the school to all stakeholders	.28	• Assures the school is in compliance with district and state mandates • Advocates on behalf of the school in the community • Advocates for the school with parents • Ensures the central office is aware of the school's accomplishments
Input	involves teachers in the design & implementation of important decisions & policies	.30	• Provides opportunity for input on all important decisions • Provides opportunities for staff to be involved in developing school policies • Uses leadership team in decision making
Affirmation	recognizes & celebrates school accomplishments & acknowledges failures	.25	• Systematically & fairly recognizes & celebrates accomplishments of teachers • Systematically & fairly recognizes & celebrates accomplishments of students • Systematically acknowledges failures & celebrates accomplishments of the school
Relationship	demonstrates an awareness of the personal aspects of teachers & staff	.19	• Remains aware of personal needs of teachers • Maintains personal relationships with teachers • Is informed about significant personal issues within the lives of staff members • Acknowledges significant events in the lives of staff members
Change agent	is willing to & actively challenges the status quo	.30	• Consciously challenges the status quo • Is comfortable with leading change initiatives with uncertain outcomes • Systematically considers new & better ways of doing things

Figure 3 (continued).
Principal Leadership Responsibilities, Average r, and Leadership Practices

Responsibilities	The extent to which the principal …	Avg r	Practices associated with responsibilities
Optimizer	inspires & leads new & challenging innovations	.20	• Inspires teachers to accomplish things that might seem beyond their grasp • Portrays a positive attitude about the ability of the staff to accomplish substantial things • Is a driving force behind major initiatives
Ideals/beliefs	communicates & operates from strong ideals & beliefs about schooling	.25	• Holds strong professional beliefs about schools, teaching, & learning • Shares beliefs about schools, teaching, & learning with the staff • Demonstrates behaviors that are consistent with beliefs
Monitors/ evaluates	monitors the effectiveness of school practices & their impact on student learning	.28	• Monitors & evaluates the effectiveness of curriculum, instruction, and assessment
Flexibility	adapts his or her leadership behavior to the needs of the current situation & is comfortable with dissent	.22	• Is comfortable with major changes in how things are done • Encourages people to express opinions contrary to those with authority • Adapts leadership style to needs of specific situations • Can be directive or non-directive as the situation warrants
Situational awareness	is aware of the details & undercurrents in the running of the school & uses this information to address current & potential problems	.33	• Is aware of informal groups & relationships among staff of the school • Is aware of issues in the school that have not surfaced but could create discord • Can predict what could go wrong from day to day
Intellectual stimulation	ensures faculty & staff are aware of the most current theories & practices & makes the discussion of these a regular aspect of the school's culture	.32	• Keeps informed about current research & theory regarding effective schooling • Continually exposes the staff to cutting-edge ideas about how to be effective • Systematically engages staff in discussions about current research & theory • Continually involves the staff in reading articles & books about effective practices

Figure 4. Differential Impact of Leadership

Range	Correlation	Change from 50th P for 1 SD Increase in Leadership
Mean	.25	60th
Highest	.50	69th
Lowest	-.02	49th

Figure 5. School and Teacher Practices Correlated with Student Achievement

School practices	1. Opportunity to learn	Agreement in the school on what students are to learn. This agreement is reflected in a curriculum taught by all of the teachers in the school.
	2. Time	The agreed-on curriculum can be taught in the time allotted for instruction.
	3. Monitoring	There are learning goals for classes of students as well as individual students.
	4. Pressure to achieve	The school communicates the importance of academic achievement. This message is supported by parents and teachers.
	5. Parental involvement	Parents are involved in developing and supporting key policies and practices in the school.
	6. School climate	Policies and procedures are in place and are clearly communicated to students and parents regarding a safe and orderly environment.
	7. Cooperation	Norms and guidelines are established and communicated for staff members working together in groups.
Teacher Practices	8. Instructional strategies	Teachers use research-based instructional strategies.
	9. Classroom management	Teachers communicate and enforce rules for general classroom conduct, seatwork, out-of-seat activities, group work, and classroom procedures.
	10. Classroom curriculum design	Teachers identify learning goals, essential versus nonessential learning for students, and organize their instructional units in a sequential or hierarchical manner when appropriate.

2. It requires individuals or groups of stakeholders to learn new approaches.

3. It conflicts with prevailing values and norms.

To the degree that individuals and/or stakeholder groups in the school or school system hold conflicting values, seek different norms, have different knowledge, or operate with varying mental models of schooling, a proposed change might represent a first-order change for some and a second-order change for others.

Figure 6. Characteristics of First- and Second-Order Changes

First-Order Change	Second-Order Change
An extension of the past	A break with the past
Within existing paradigms	Outside of existing paradigms
Consistent with prevailing values and norms	Conflicted with prevailing values and norms
Incremental	Complex
Implemented with existing knowledge & skills	Requires new knowledge & skills to implement
Implemented by experts	Implemented by stakeholders

Different perceptions about the implications of change can lead to one person's solution becoming someone else's problem. That is, if a change has first-order implications for one person or group of individuals, yet has second-order implications for another person or group, this latter group may view the change as a problem rather than a solution. Research has shown this is true of nearly every educational reform introduced over the last 20 years. The shift from focusing on the inputs of schooling to the outputs of schooling, which was the core concept in "outcome-based" education, is a classic and dramatic example of one person's solution being someone else's problem.

Many more current examples of first-order changes exist for some educators, policy makers, and parents, including the role and use of content standards; high-stakes testing and accountability; adjustments in school days, weeks, and years; non-graded classrooms; home schooling; and school vouchers. They are appropriate responses to what educators, policy makers, and parents see as problems with schools. These "solutions" are consistent with their prevailing values and norms and are seen as natural extensions of their ongoing efforts to improve schools.

Other educators, policy makers, and parents, however, may see such changes as dramatic and undesirable breaks with the past, which conflict sharply with their prevailing values and norms. In short, they are viewed as second-order changes. That is, instead of being viewed as solutions, many see them as problems facing schools and school systems, which have far greater implications for students and stakeholder groups than those problems currently facing the schools.

Recognizing which changes are first and second order for which individuals and stakeholder groups helps leaders to select leadership practices and strategies appropriate for their initiatives. Doing so enhances the likelihood of sustainable initiatives and a positive impact on achievement. Failing to do so, on the other hand, can result in changes having a marginal or negative impact on achievement.

Continuing Research and Development

Our research and development on the topic of educational leadership continues. Our ultimate objective is to increase the accessibility, utility, and applicability of research for educational leaders. To this end, we are collecting data from current principals so we can complete a factor analysis of the 21 leadership responsibilities. We suspect several of them are highly interrelated. A factor analysis will allow us to "tease out" any interrelationships that do exist and reduce the number of responsibilities to what may be a more manageable set. We also continue to review research studies for possible inclusion in our meta-analysis. If future iterations of our reports reflect slight variations in our correlations, these will be a result of our ongoing research.

When we have completed our factor analysis, we will correlate the resulting factors to the Interstate School Leaders Licensure Consortium (ISLLC) standards for administrator preparation. This correlation may enhance the connection of the current standards with quantitative research, as well as identify knowledge and skills critical to effective education leadership that are not covered or addressed in these standards.

In addition to our analysis of the quantitative research on principal leadership, we are synthesizing the theoretical literature in the areas of living systems, organizational learning, change and change management, transition management, and leadership. We believe the theoretical and procedural knowledge developed in these domains can be of great value to practitioners to effectively meet the 21 leadership responsibilities and engage in the 66 leadership practices found in quantitative research. Currently, if school leaders wish to improve their practices through the use of the knowledge in these domains, they must seek and determine the knowledge that should be applied to the 66 practices, at what time, and in what ways. It is hoped our synthesis will make it easier for leaders to incorporate this knowledge into their practices.

The Value of This Research for Principals, Superintendents, and Policy Makers

We anticipate this research will be valuable to all concerned with educational leadership. For principals, it provides clarity and specificity about the leadership practices with the strongest relationships to student achievement. We have read for years about the importance of instructional leadership. Now we can quantify the effect of leadership on student achievement and school productivity. Moreover, we can define instructional leadership in terms of responsibilities and practices that if done well produce results, rather than in terms of personality traits or leadership styles. In addition, we are now able to design preparation and professional development programs to address the specific responsibilities and practices principals need in order to make the positive effect on achievement the research indicates they could be making.

Superintendents will find ways to use this research as well. The superintendents with whom we are working already have begun to use our findings in their recruitment and selection process. Interviews with prospective principals include questions about what candidates know and how they approach their leadership responsibilities and practices. Superintendents also are using this research as the basis for designing supervision and professional development programs for current principals. Some have said they are eager to begin using these responsibilities and practices in the performance appraisal/evaluation processes.

State and local board members who approve administrator preparation, professional development, and licensure have also expressed interest in this work. They now have additional research on which to base decisions about preparation and licensure program approval. When we complete our factor analysis and the correlation of our factors to the ISLLC standards, policy makers will have the data they need if they wish to approve and/or review programs based on standards *and* on research.

Final Thoughts

We have come a long way since the early days of effective schools research. The recent push for increased evidence of "what works" is helping to define a "new science" of education. This new science of education is being built, to some degree, on the shoulders of the pioneers of effective schools research. We hope our efforts honor their dedication, determination, commitment, and leadership to better serve *all* of America's children through ubiquitous, high-quality, effective education.

References

Beckard, R., & Pritchard, W. (1992). *Changing the essence: The art of creating and leading fundamental change in organizations.* San Francisco: Jossey-Bass.

Bridges, W. (1991). *Managing transitions: Making the most of change.* Reading, MA: Addison-Wesley.

Brookover, W.B., & Lezotte, L.W. (1979). *Changes in school characteristics coincident with changes in student achievement.* East Lansing: Institute for Research on Teaching, Michigan State University. (ERIC Document Reproduction Service No. ED 181 005)

Edmonds, R.R. (1979, October). Effective schools for the urban poor. *Educational Leadership, 37,* 15–27.

Elmore, R. (2003). *Knowing the right thing to do: School improvement and performance-based accountability.* Washington, DC: NGA Center for Best Practices.

Fullan, M.G. (1993). *Change forces: Probing the depths of educational reform.* Bristol, PA: Falmer Press.

Glenn, B.C. (1981). *What works? An examination of effective schools for poor black children.* Cambridge, MA: Center for Law and Education, Harvard University.

Heifetz, R. (1994). *Leadership without easy answers.* Cambridge, MA: Belknap Press.

Hesselbein, F., & Johnston, R. (Eds.). (2002). *On leading change: A leader to leader guide.* San Francisco: Jossey-Bass.

Kanter, R.M. (1985). *Change masters: Innovations for productivity in the American corporation* (Reprint ed.). New York: Free Press.

Marzano, R.J. (1998). *A theory-based meta-analysis of research on instruction.* Aurora, CO: Mid-continent Research for Education and Learning.

Marzano, R.J. (2000). *A new era of school reform: Going where the research takes us.* Aurora, CO: Mid-continent Research for Education and Learning.

Marzano, R.J., Pickering, D.J., & Pollock, J.E. (2001). *Classroom instruction that works: Research-based strategies for increasing student achievement.* Alexandria, VA: Association for Supervision and Curriculum Development.

Nadler, D.A., Shaw, R.B., Walton, A.E., & Associates. (1994). *Discontinuous change.* San Francisco: Jossey-Bass.

Rogers, E. (1995). *Diffusion of innovations.* New York: Free Press.

Weber, G. (1971). *Inner-city children can be taught to read: Four successful schools.* Washington, DC: Council for Basic Education.

Related Resources

Marzano, R.J. (2003). *What works in schools: Translating research into action.* Alexandria, VA: Association for Supervision and Curriculum Development.

Marzano, R.J., Gaddy, B.B., & Dean, C. (2000). *What works in classroom instruction.* Aurora, CO: Mid-continent Research for Education and Learning.

(Editor's Note: A bibliography of the 70 research studies included in the McREL leadership meta-analysis is available on request by contacting the authors at McREL, 2550 S. Parker Road, Suite 500, Aurora, CO 80014. Phone: 303-337-0990.)

Tim Waters, Ed.D., is CEO, Robert J. Marzano, Ph.D., is senior scholar, and Brian McNulty, Ph.D., is vice president for field services, all of McREL.

Tim Waters, Ed.D., is CEO, Robert J. Marzano, Ph.D., is senior scholar, and Brian McNulty, Ph.D., is vice president for field services, all of McREL.

Chapter 6: Questions for Reflection and Discussion

1. In this meta-analysis, 66 leadership practices embedded within 21 leadership responsibilities were identified, each with statistically significant correlations to student achievement. They are summarized on p. 77-79. To put this material into a real-life context, evaluate your own performance in relation to these practices.

2. Examine the leadership practices in relation to a mentor you had in the past. What did you observe to be the practices that were the most critical to this person's success?

3. Review the list of characteristics of first- and second-order changes given on p. 81. Consider the changes currently underway in your district and decide whether they are first- or second-order.

4. To what extent are these changes solving a problem vs. changing the locus of the problem? And what action would you recommend?

7 Preparing Principals for Leadership Success

Patricia Lindauer, Garth Petrie, John Leonard, John Gooden, and Brenda Bennett

As school administrators rely more heavily on staff members, faculty, parents, and others to help them initiate and sustain school excellence, they must be proficient in conflict resolution and consensus-building skills, as well as other communication and group-process skills. But how prepared are they in these areas?

This article reports two research studies and summarizes findings from and between the two. The authors point out the disparity of function between theory and practice as it applies to the preparation and need for small-group process skills in school leadership. Use of such skills is documented weekly by principals, with little or poor preparation in such skills identified. The authors call for the professorate and educational leaders to work together to improve preparation programs in this area.

The obsolete concept of the school administrator as a relatively passive manager has given way to a more accurate view of the educational administrator as an active leader involved in instructional concerns, personnel issues, and management considerations (Pavan 1991). Gardner (1990) expands this thinking when he states that no single individual has all the skills nor the time to carry out all the complex tasks of contemporary leadership. Tubbs (1992) posits that few leaders can succeed today without committed and competent team members. These challenges and their concomitant responses are often complex; ranging from resolving explosive family conflicts to implementing new state or federal legislation. Clearly, technical skill alone is insufficient, as is a complete reliance on content knowledge. The heart of professional active leadership lies between these two poles (Feyerherm 1994). Supporting this complexity, Black and English (1986) point out that priority in administrative preparation programs should be given to generalizable knowledge and skills that can address new situations as well as traditional patterns. According to Bradford and Cohen (1984), the solution that worked yesterday is only slightly appropriate today and will be irrelevant tomorrow.

Evidence accumulated from research, coupled with widespread recent concern about the quality of American Education, has contributed to a renewed interest in the important role school administrators play in initiating and sustaining school excellence (Gooden, Petrie, Lindauer, & Richardson 1998). Yet current practices for selecting, preparing, and rewarding school administrators do not always identify and develop needed competence (Matthews and Beeson 1991). Much of this preparation is widely believed to be out of touch with reality—irrelevant, out of date, abstract, theoretical, course-driven, and impractical.

Almost every administrator organization has published a report highlighting the important role school administrators play in initiating and sustaining school excellence and the need for the development of future administrators (Murphy 1990). The newest standards developed by the Interstate School Leaders Licensure Consortium (ISLLC), *Standards for School Leaders*, include such standards as: 1) use of effective problem-framing and problem-solving skills; 2) use of effective conflict resolution skills; 3) use of effective group-process and consensus-building skills; and, 4) use of effective communication skills. This reconstituted emphasis on creating better preparation programs will change the face of American education, particularly higher education, which must respond to most of these demands for change (Hallinger and Hausman 993).

One of the primary areas of concern relates to group-process skills (Organ and Bateman 1996). Whether or not the administrator wishes to understand or to work effectively with others, it is necessary to know a great deal about the nature of groups, particularly the psychological and social forces associated with groups and group behavior (Gresso and Robertson 1992). As more schools and school districts move toward participatory decision making, or at least site-based management, the importance of understanding human behavior in groups has been exacerbated for the principal (Hallinger and Richardson 1988; Lindauer 1993).

Definition

Tubbs (1992) believes modern organizations are being radically transformed to better utilize human potential, primarily through the use of small groups, and has identified one of the key skills or attributes of a quality principal as expertise in group process. Alderfer (1987) also maintains that group process is a key element in the job responsibilities of the school administrator. While the school administrator certainly spends considerable time in one-on-one contacts with people, the contact with groups often requires even more time (Fiol 1994). Effective leaders must not only have knowledge of groups, but must use group-process leadership skills to work effectively to accomplish the organizational goals. Cragan and Wright (1991) define small group process skills as "a few people involved in communication interaction over time, ... who have common goals and norms and have developed a communication pattern for meeting their goals in an interdependent manner" (7).

The problems addressed in this report were not so much agreement on the need for group-process preparation, but on the need for inclusion of group-process skill development in the preparation programs for school administrators (Lindauer, Petrie and Gooden in press). Seldom are there courses, the university's usual method of delivery, that are designed to prepare potential leaders in group process skills. Even more alarming is the lack of resources that directly address the school administrator's role in facilitating and developing groups (Blackwell 1988; Forsyth 1990; Gresso and Robertson 1992; Sagie 1994).

An understanding of the different types of groups found within the local school will enable the principal to begin the process of developing effective leadership skills in working with these groups (Smith and Smith 1994). Knowledge of group process will enable the principal to focus energy on the productivity of school constituents as well as on its clients (Lindauer, Petrie, and Gooden 1998). Key to the development of effective skills in understanding and working with these groups is the attainment of knowledge on group behavior, the use of synergy as a leadership tool, and the use of learning as a means of focusing the different groups on positive goals (Richardson, Lane, Granger, and Gooden, 1995; Salas, Prince, Baker, and Shrestha 1995; Wanous, Reichers, Cooper, and Rao 1994).

The questions addressed by these two studies were: With an evident paucity of productive preparation for group-process skills development, how are school leaders coping with an area that appears so important to their professional lives? Secondly, and perhaps more importantly, are principals trying to cope without the use of such skills?

Method

Subjects

To obtain the information needed to answer the questions guiding this study, surveys were sent to 200 randomly selected Georgia and 200 randomly selected Kentucky elementary, middle, and high school principals. The Georgia surveys had 108 (54 percent) of the principals responding. After the Kentucky surveys were disseminated, 154 (76 percent) of the principals responded.

Instrumentation

The authors developed a 25-item, Likert-formatted questionnaire, with one (1) meaning "none" and five (5) meaning "extensive." An expert review panel piloted the questionnaire to establish reliability and validity. A coefficient of 0.87 was determined using the Cronbach reliability test. The first part of the questionnaire consisted of items requesting demographic information so that data could be utilized in a variety of configurations to test the differences between variables (i.e. gender, experience, etc.). The second part consisted of 13 questions that dealt with principals' acquiring and using group process skills. See Table 1.

Data Analysis

All data were entered into a database and statistical treatments were performed using the SPSS system. The data were then organized, and demographic variables were used as sources of independent variables for descriptive purposes. Inferential analyses were also run for exploratory purposes based on the demographic variables (Gay 1996).

Results

The Georgia data revealed that respondents' experience in administration ranged from one to 27 years. The data also indicated that 56 percent of the respondents were male and 44 percent female. A majority of the respondents were from Georgia's urban districts (32 percent), with most working in schools with a student population of more than 1,000. The school configurations included K-4, K-5, 5-8, and 9-12, with a few other combinations. Staff size ranged from nine to the largest school reporting a staff of more than 100 members. The number of assistant principals ranged from zero to five. Teaching staffs in the reporting schools were described by the responding principals as young and inexperienced to having more than 10 years of experience, with most holding master's degrees.

The Kentucky data revealed that 73 of the returns represented some form of K-4, K-5 or 5-8 configuration, with the remainder representing various 7-12 configurations of which 9-12 was the most common. Most of the Kentucky principals were from rural or rural-urban schools that ranged in size from 300 to 500 students. Of the respondents, 29.5 percent were female and 70.5 percent male. Teaching staffs ranged in size from eight to more than 100, and the number of assistant principals ranged from zero to four. Experience in administration ranged from one to 27 years, with the average experience being 9.88 years. The number of years to retirement ranged from 0 to 26 years, with 71 (46 percent) indicating they would retire within five years and 88 (57 percent) saying they plan to retire within seven years.

The description of management style for both the Kentucky and Georgia principals ranged from top-down management to strongly collaborative, with a variety of combinations of top-down and collaborative. In the Kentucky group, 129 indicated that their school was actively using site-based management (SBDM), and 23 indicated their school was not an active SBDM school. Only 17 percent of the Georgia principals who responded indicated they were actively engaged in site-based programs.

Mean data revealed that a majority of the respondents from both states have positive feelings about group-process skills (GA = 4.00, KY = 4.36). They also believe that learning these skills is essential and necessary for ultimate job success (GA = 4.14, KY = 4.57). However, they felt they had received little formal training (GA = 3.48, KY = 2.46) and that their preparation was of relatively poor quality (GA = 3.58, KY = 3.53). See Table 1.

When queried about usage of group-process skills, the Georgia respondents gave the highest mean ratings to establishing climate (3.97) and consensus building (3.68), while Kentucky principals gave the highest mean ratings to agenda setting (4.64) and trust building (4.57). All the Kentucky respondents indicated that there was a need for group-process skills training for administrators (5.00), and nearly all indicated they would recommend such training to a colleague (4.68). Georgia principals felt less of a need (3.42) to recommend group-process training to a colleague. See Table 1.

When Kentucky administrators were asked if they believed universities should do more to help new administrators develop group process skills, seven respondents said "no" and 147 answered "yes". This answer was reinforced by both groups of respondents when they indicated most had learned their group-process skills outside the university and by indications of where they had seen such skills modeled. When asked about the development of their group-process skills, respondents indicated that the majority learned their skills through their own self improvement (GA: N = 66, KY: N = 119). Only 30 Georgia and 54 Kentucky respondents indicated that they had learned any portion of their group-process skills through college classes. See Table 1 for the complete description.

When asked where most group-process skills were used, the respondents from Kentucky indicated they used such skills mostly in faculty settings, and with parents and students to a lesser degree. Georgia principals gave the same responses, listing faculty settings, parent groups, and students, in that order. See Table 1 for more detail.

Concerning where practicing principals have seen group-process skills modeled, the professorate received low marks. The Georgia respondents gave professors the lowest ranking of the four choices (N = 28), while giving colleagues the highest rating (N = 59). The Kentucky respondents were of the same mind and gave the professorate an even lower rating (N = 19), with colleagues receiving the highest rating (N = 86). In both cases, supervisors and teachers fell between the professorate and colleagues. See the table for a complete listing.

Discussion

Traditionally, preparation programs for school administrators represent individual universities and school districts working as separate entities. With the exception of an occasional university faculty member serving as a guest speaker for a group of aspiring school administrators, or the practitioner speaking to the university class, each organization articulates a separate vision and thus different programs (Smith and Smith 1994). The researchers believe this disparity of function between the two has led to a need for university program revision.

Quite often the principal operates in a SBDM setting as a micro-superintendent, with a school council acting much the same as a district school board (Matthews

Table 1. Principals' group-process skills responses

	Georgia			Kentucky		
	M	SD	n	M	SD	n
Value attached to group process skills	4.00	1.41		4.36	1.42	
Importance of skills to job success	4.14	1.39		4.57	1.27	
Amount of training in group process	3.48	1.46		2.46	1.41	
Quality of training in group process	3.58	2.54		3.53	2.51	
Use of group process skills per week	3.27	1.40		3.38	2.68	
Skills used:						
a. Team building	3.68	2.42		3.37	1.42	
b. Trust building	3.69	2.40		4.57	1.27	
c. Consensus building	3.68	2.42		4.42	1.41	
d. Agenda setting	3.45	2.50		4.64	1.29	
e. Establishing climate	3.97	1.29		4.25	1.48	
f. Conducting meetings	3.68	2.42		4.54	1.29	
Need for group process skills to be taught	00	(not asked)		5.00	1.41	
Recommend training	3.42	1.46		4.68	1.29	
Level of your proficiency in group process skills	3.48	1.48		4.40	1.41	
Where group process skills learned:						
a. On my own			66			119
b. Workshops			62			108
c. Professional development			53			111
d. College			30			54
e. Natural talent			35			58
Settings in which group process skills used:						
a. Faculty			90			131
b. Community			51			76
c. Parents			60			91
d. Administrative groups			55			81
e. Students			60			90
Group process skills modeled by:						
a. Colleagues			59			86
b. Professors			28			19
c. Supervisors			42			42
d. Teachers			49			49

Note: Numbers are more than 100% due to multiple responses.
Georgia: N = 108, Kentucky: N = 154.

and Beeson 1991). In today's environment more actors are involved in the school; parents, community members, students, faculty, and staff are invited and encouraged to participate in making decisions that affect them and the school (Richardson et al. 1995). Yet preparation in group-process skills is not considered a requirement for preservice principals who must deal with these diverse groups.

The respondents in the two studies reported that group-process skills were critical to their job success, that they would recommend training for their colleagues, that they attached value to group-process skills, and that they believed there was a need for group-process skill training for administrators. In spite of these positive attitudes, the respondents felt the amount of training they had was relatively limited and that the quality of that training was mediocre at best. Still, more than half of the respondents used group-process skills weekly and indicated that they had a relatively high degree of proficiency in group-process skills. But where did they learn these skills? The respondents basically said that they learned them somewhere other than in preparation programs vis-a-vis the university. This is a scathing indictment of the lack of congruence between theoretical and practical worlds.

Conclusions

The respondents represented a 10 percent sample of the nearly 1,500 principals in Kentucky and 1,800 principals in Georgia. With sufficient principal responses, the findings of these studies lead the researchers to the following conclusions. First, group-process skills are an important tool for practicing school principals, especially where school-based decision making (SBDM) is the driving force in school restructuring.

Secondly, the amount of training and the quality of that training are inadequate at best and too haphazard at worst. Such skills need to be included in both professional development programs being designed for practicing principals and in preservice preparation programs designed for aspiring principals.

Thirdly, the group-process skills practicing principals have acquired are not developed in university preparation programs or through university-related professional development efforts. The respondents felt that university preparation programs were the least likely place for such skills to be modeled and learned. If this is indeed the case, then perhaps educational leadership professors need to revisit existing preparation programs. After all, university programs are supposed to be on the cutting edge of the improvement curve. Could it be that we have forgotten that a major, second order (Cuban 1988), change is going on in the public and private schools of the nation and that new skills are called for if practicing principals are to be successful leaders of that change?

A fourth and more troublesome finding is that the high level of relationship between group-process skills and a principal's perceived job success creates a disparity of function between theory and practice. Because university leadership programs and school systems work with distinctly different agendas, the requirements and expectations often are less unified. In other words, the two lack common goals and purposes.

Fifth, there is an overwhelming need, expressed by the respondents, for universities to do more, and this seems to the authors to be a clarion call for action; to develop such skills in their programs. If such programs are not forthcoming it leaves one to wonder who will fill the vacuum, for it is a surety that the vacuum will be filled.

Sixth, it appears that in SBDM settings, principals have greater need for group-process training than in traditional programs. At least greater percentages of the Kentucky respondents indicated that they used and needed such preparation. Also, the Kentucky respondents were more adamant about the need for universities to provide that training.

Seventh, where left on their own in voluntary SBDM settings, it appears that females are more likely to seek and obtain skills in group process than their male counterparts. They also feel more confident that they can use such skills.

Finally, and in response to the two questions guiding the studies, school administrators are coping with the group-process skills dilemma. However, they are doing so with minimal training, which they classify as inadequate and which was acquired outside the traditional preparation program menu, i.e., the university setting.

While this study has addressed the needs of school principals, the needs do not stop there. Black and English (1986) have stated: "The higher up the administrative career ladder one goes, the more the administrator deals with groups," pointing out that principals' need for group-process skills is only the first step up the ladder (18). If true, the need for inclusion of group-process skills training at the university level, especially in professional development programs, is urgent and widespread.

References

Alderfer, C. P. (Ed.). (1987). *An intergroup perspective on group dynamics*. Englewood Cliffs, NJ: Prentice-Hall.

Black, J. A., & English, F. W. (1986). *What they don't tell you in schools of education about school administration*. Lancaster, PA: Technomic Publishing Company.

Bradford, D. L., & Cohen, A. R. (1984). *Managing for excellence: The guide to developing high performance in contemporary organizations*. New York, NY: Wiley.

Cragan, J., & Wright, D. (1991). *Communication on small groups: Theory, process, skills*. (4th ed.). New York: West Publishing.

Cuban, L. (1988). A fundamental puzzle of school reform. *Phi Delta Kappan, 69*(5), 341-344.

Feyerherm, A. E. (1994). Leadership in collaboration: A longitudinal study of two interorganizational rule-making groups. *Leadership Quarterly, 5*(3-4), 253-270.

Fiol, C. M. (1994). Consensus, diversity, and learning in organizations. *Organization Science, 5*(3), 403-420.

Forsyth, D. R. (1990). *Group Dynamics*. (2nd ed.). Pacific Grove, CA: Brooks/Cole Publishing Company.

Gooden, J., Petrie, G., Lindauer, P., & Richardson, M. (1988). Principals' needs for small-group process skills. *NASSP Bulletin, 82*(596), 102-107.

Gresso, D. W., & Robertson, M. B. (1992). The principal as process consultant: Catalyst for change. *NASSP Bulletin, 76*(540), 44-48.

Gay, L. (1996). *Educational research competencies for analysis and application*. (5th ed.) Englewood Cliffs, New Jersey: Prentice-Hall.

Hallinger, P., & Hausman, C. (1993, April). *From Attila the Hun to Mary Had a Little Lamb*. Paper presented at the American Educational Research Association in Atlanta, GA.

Hallinger, P., & Richardson, D. (1988, April). *Models of shared leadership: Evolving structures and relationships*. Paper presented at the American Educational Research Association in New Orleans, LA.

Lindauer, P. (1993). Principal leadership effectiveness and school-based council effectiveness as perceived by teachers. Unpublished doctoral dissertation. Carbondale, IL: Southern Illinois University.

Lindauer, P., Petrie, G., & Gooden, J. (1988). Needed: Group process skills for principals. *Educational Research Quarterly, 22*(2).

Matthews, R. J., & Beeson, G. W. (1991, April). *Emerging power and leadership: The developing role of new principals in Australia*. Paper presented at the American Educational Research Association in Chicago, IL.

Murphy, J. (1990). Preparing school administrators for the twenty-first century: The reform agenda. In B. Mitchell & L. Cunningham (Eds). *Educational leadership and changing contexts of families, communities, and schools*. Chicago: University of Chicago Press.

Organ, D. W., & Bateman, T. (1996). *Organizational behavior*. (3rd ed.). Plano, TX: Business Publications.

Pavan, B. N. (1991, April,). *Principal change facilitator styles and the implementation of instructional support teams*. Paper presented at the American Educational Research Association in Chicago, IL. (ERIC Document Reproduction Service No. ED 339138)

Richardson, M. D., Lane, K. E., Granger, M. W., & Gooden, J. S. (1995, November). *Principal Preparation: Focus on group process skills*. Paper presented at the Southern Regional Council on Education Administration in Memphis, TN.

Sagie, A. (1994). Participative decision making and performance: A moderator analysis. *Journal of Applied Behavioral Science, 30*(2), 227-246.

Salas, E., Prince, C., Baker, D. P., & Shrestha, L. (1995). Situation awareness in term performance: Implications for measurement and training. *Human Factors, 37*(1), 123-136.

Smith, A. J., & Smith, I. G. (1994). The process of management education: An innovative approach to outcomes evaluation. *Management Learning, 25*(4), 527-542.

Tubbs, S. L. (1992). *A systems approach to small group interaction*. (4th ed.). New York, NY: McGraw Hill.

Wanous, J. P., Reichers, A. E., Cooper, C., & Rao, R. (1994). Effectiveness of problem-solving groups: Process and outcome criteria. *Psychological Reports, 75*(3), 1139-1153.

Patricia Lindauer, Ph.D., is an associate professor, Garth Petrie, Ph.D., is a professor, and John Leonard, Ph.D., is an assistant professor, all of secondary education and educational leadership at Stephen F. Austin State University; John Gooden, Ph.D., is a professor of educational leadership at Alabama State University; Brenda Bennett is an instructor of medical technology at Henderson Community College, Henderson, Ky.

Chapter 7: Questions for Reflection and Discussion

1. In examining the complexity of the leader's role, the authors cite a source to the effect that administrative preparation programs should give priority to generalizable knowledge and skills that can address new situations as well as traditional ones. What advice would you give to university graduate programs trying to address this priority?

2. This article identifies "expertise in group process" as one of the key skills of a school administrator. In reviewing events in your school over the past year, to what extent would this type of expertise have likely led to different outcomes? Were there events in which these skills were present but did not affect the outcome?

3. Most respondents in this survey considered their training in group-process skills limited and its quality mediocre, although they considered the skills important. In reflecting on your own group-process skills, would you consider the training you've had to be good? What sources do you consider the most productive in learning group-process skills?

8 Indiana Study Explores Link Between Patterns of Leadership Behavior and Administrator Stress

Bobby G. Malone and Jacquelyn S. Nelson

The responsibility for the academic success of our nation's children historically has been shouldered by the school principal. In many school communities today, that accountability has been mandated by state law.

The Indiana equivalent of the accountability movement sweeping the nation is Public Law 221 (P.L. 221), which makes the principal solely responsible for the continuous improvement of the schools. The time needed to accomplish the academic goals required by the new legislation, however, often is compromised by the principal's involvement in non-academic duties. Issues such as collective bargaining, control over staff development activities, and the disciplining of faculty are relatively new pressures that add greatly to the principal's job, a job that already is too demanding and stressful. With the addition of the new legal requirement, managing stress will become a larger part of the principal's everyday duties if he or she is to remain healthy and productive.

Leadership is an essential ingredient in how well principals cope with their responsibilities. The purpose of this study was to investigate the relationship between principals' leadership behavior and their on-the-job stress. Stress has been identified as one of the most serious barriers to entering the principalship (Malone, Sharp, and Thompson 2000). Combined with a dearth of qualified candidates and projected shortages in applicants for principal positions through 2008, a thorough understanding of this situation is crucial to the long-term survival of U.S. public schools. A secondary purpose of this study was to investigate differences in leadership style between men and women in the principalship.

Job experience, school size, and gender were used as variables to analyze data collected from high school principals in Indiana.

Responses from 162 of 239 principals of high schools housing grades 9 through 12 were analyzed. No significant patterns of leadership behavior were linked to the two types of stress that were investigated, and leadership behavior did not differ significantly by gender.

Today's high school principals face extraordinary challenges in guiding, shaping, and preparing America's young people for productive lives in the new millennium. Growing incidents of violence such as those that occurred in Paducah, Ky., and Littleton, Colo., bear grave evidence to the societal problems that have crept into U.S. schools. Along with witnessing increased aggressive teenage behavior, educational leaders experience long working hours, high volumes of paperwork, conflict with teachers, lack of adequate resources, role ambiguity, lack of support from supervisors and the public, and rapid changes such as the growing necessity of providing the latest technological innovations for students (Hanson 1996; Cedoline 1982; Gmelch 1978). Principals must also contend with unqualified teachers, rapid shifts in student populations, increased special education requirements, legal issues, the poor image and status of the education profession, and pressures to improve student achievement. These issues have been identified as major sources of job-related stress that have caused educators to turn away from the principalship (Koschnick 2002).

A sample of school superintendents reported that, due to the above problems, there is a shortage of qualified candidates for principal openings, a trend that is projected to increase through 2008 (Educational Research Service 1998). The shortage problem is compounded by the fact that large numbers of principals are projected to retire and small numbers of individuals are enrolling in principal preparation programs. The shortage of administrators is exacerbated further by large numbers of current principals leaving the profession for reasons other than retirement. Job stress could be the most important. Milstein and Farkas (1988) found that one-fourth of the 1,600 principals in their study planned to leave the education profession because of stress-related burnout. Earlier, Gmelch and Torelli (1993) found a high correlation (.70) between what they termed task-based stress and administrator exhaustion. Leader burnout, coupled with existing and projected shortages, serves to place the principalship in a state of jeopardy.

Principal Accountability and Stress

In a secondary educational institution, principals are accountable for all that occurs in a school. These instructional leaders experience considerable stress as they cope with a large number of problems that seem almost insurmountable (Institute of Educational Leadership 2000). Principals are expected to increase student achievement, improve teacher efficiency, and work toward collaborative decisions with staff and parents (Brimm 1983; Gmelch 1978). Fullan stated in his study of Saskatchewan principals, "Perhaps no area of education imposes more stress than the public school principalship. Confrontation, conflict, and compromise are constants which principals face on a daily basis" (as cited in Yackel 1984, 84). It has been estimated that 80 percent of the principal's day is spent in direct contact with people (Cedoline 1982), confronting societal issues such as child abuse and neglect, drug and alcohol abuse, single-parent families, and child custody situations. These increased time requirements place educators on an emotional roller coaster (Banach 2001) that even more than 20 years ago pushed them to the point of burnout (Cedoline 1982). School leaders face verbal abuse from teachers and parents when the parties disagree with administrators' decisions. Most administrators are trained to deal with student conflict and aggression, but dealing with parental and personnel acts of aggression and threats is relatively new (Sternberg 2000). Today, more than four in 10 principals are being driven out of educational leadership positions because of unreasonable standards and pressures of accountability (Johnson 2002).

One of the emerging issues related to the stressfulness of the principal's job is conflict with teachers. With the preponderance of collective bargaining and teacher unions, many issues previously thought to be nonnegotiable are now on the bargaining table. Dealing with a teacher who is not performing his or her job can be an unpleasant experience, and such situations may be complicated by the teacher's affiliation with the local teachers' association. Koschnick (2002) found the issue of disciplining teachers to be a growing phenomenon and a growing source of stress for high school principals.

Review of Related Literature

The concepts of leadership behavior are complex. The study of leadership has evolved over the past half-century as investigators have attempted to ascertain the characteristics or behaviors necessary for strong and effective administrators. An early scale, the *Leader Behavior Description Questionnaire* (LBDQ 1945), was developed to describe various leader behaviors. From studies using this instrument, leadership characteristics were categorized into combinations of behaviors termed "initiating structure" or "consideration" (Hersey and Blanchard 1982). Bales (1953) postulated there were two types of leaders: "task-oriented," concerned with organizational function, and "social-emotional," concerned with morale and cohesiveness of the unit. Later, researchers described leadership styles very similar to those presented by Bales (Blake and Mouton 1994; Fiedler 1967; Halpin and Winer 1957). Blake and Mouton developed the Managerial Grid, now referred to as the Leadership Grid (Lunenburg and Ornstein 2000), and identified five leadership styles predicated on two essential concepts: "concern for people" and "concern for task."

There is no agreed-upon definition of leadership; it is the most-studied but least-understood phenomenon of our day (Burns 1978). Theorists differ in their opinions as to the number and types of leadership styles (Hersey and Blanchard 1982; Kouzes and Posner 1993; Kowalski 1999; McGregor 1960; Ogawa and Bossert 1995;

Sergiovanni and Elliott 1975; Stogdill 1974; Ubben and Hughes 1997). While opinions differ as to the nature of leadership, probably the most common ingredient in the professional literature is the term "influence." There may be disagreement over the specifics of leadership, but rarely is there disagreement over the essential need for a competent functioning leader if an organization is to perform at its maximum potential. When reform efforts for improving schools are presented, it is extremely rare for principals to be left out of the discussion.

Another aspect of leadership behavior is the question of differences in leadership behavior between men and women. While research on leadership behaviors of men and women in the principalship is sparse, there are studies of patterns of leadership style at the superintendent level. One area of investigation centered on leadership styles of the superintendent, how interactions are shaped, and how roles are established (Tallerico 1999). These studies have yielded contrasting opinions. Ortiz and Marshall (1988) believed that interpreting comparative studies of male and female administrators led to false assumptions that gender was a factor in differences between administrators, rather than the administrators' prior experiences. Wesson and Grady (1994) discovered females relied more on collaborative leadership practices than their male counterparts and men and women defined power differently. In contrast, most leadership theory tends to oversimplify the significance of gender. Brunner (1999) asserted that women are more collaborative in their approach as leaders, but she did not imply if this is due to gender differences or external factors such as experience, role in society, or education.

Significance of the Problem

In reviewing the literature on stress and leadership behaviors, the researchers noted a lack of recent research on the subject. Although leadership studies and stress studies are numerous, most were written many years ago and were based on opinion rather than empirical evidence. Further, few investigators have explored the concepts of leadership behavior and sources of stress.

In reviewing Koschnick's (2002) study, we perceived the need to explore the concept of leadership with different instrumentation as well as to conduct a statewide study with representative sampling strategies. If leadership behavior was measured with the Leadership Practices Inventory (LPI), emerging results could be attributed to one of the most reliable and currently used instruments for assessing leadership behavior. We also perceived a need to develop a more tightly conceived research plan for data analysis, e.g., subscales of the LPI comparisons with two categories of stress as measured by the Administrative Stress Index (ASI). The overall purpose of the study was to investigate the link between leadership behavior and perceived sources of job-related stress. Due to the dearth of research on leadership behaviors of high school principals, a supportive purpose was also to investigate the question of differences in leadership style between men and women in the principalship.

Malone, Sharp, and Thompson (2000) found that among Indiana's principals, aspiring principals, and superintendents, stress was one of the most serious barriers to entering the principalship. It is important that administrators examine not only the stress encountered during the day-to-day operations of the schools, but also how they recognize and deal with stress (Brock and Grady 2002). Because stress can cause serious health concerns, an evaluation of how principals' leadership behavior is affected by the increasing demands and expectations of their jobs is crucial to the survival of schools. The study also will serve to enlighten current and prospective educators by evaluating their abilities to enter this challenging profession. Educators need to be well prepared for the challenges of the 21st century. Investigating the effect of stress on leadership behavior will be useful in developing coping strategies for the training of qualified individuals for the nation's schools. An understanding of this phenomenon is important in order to stem the flow of administrators away from leadership positions.

In the Effective Schools Research (Edmonds 1979), the principal is viewed as the essential ingredient in school improvement. This is especially true in Indiana. Current legislation (P.L. 221)—called "the accountability bill"—places the responsibility for school improvement directly on the principal. With the passage of this law, a new stage of school reform was initiated. The bill passed the Indiana legislature in 2001 with clear expectations that public schools were to improve in at least three selected measures of student achievement, e.g., Indiana Statewide Testing for Educational Progress (ISTEP+), graduation rates for high schools, and dropout rates for high schools. School personnel have been encouraged to collect data about their schools in a systematic manner in order to compare progress from year to year. Key wording in the legislation is "continuous improvement," and the responsibility for the school's improvement lies squarely on the principal. Such responsibility has a price and could very well constitute additional demands on an already stressful job. With this added responsibility and the fact that schools face a shortage of principal candidates, as well as increasing numbers of principals retiring, an investigation of the issues facing Indiana principals is timely.

Research Methods

Instruments. This study was conducted via mailed survey. Two instruments were used in collecting the data: the Leadership Practices Inventory (LPI), developed in 1997 to collect data from principals about their leadership practices, and the Administrative Stress Index (ASI) as developed by Gmelch and Torelli (1993) to collect data about principals' task-oriented stress or relationship-oriented stress. The LPI, originally developed by Kouzes and Posner in the late 1970s, was carefully planned and extensively developed, and is probably the most-used instrument in leadership studies and training today.

The ASI was designed to measure perceived job-related stress. Swent and Gmelch developed the instrument in a 1977 study of principals in Oregon. The 35-item original questionnaire was pared down to its current 20-item format through a series of successive studies (Gmelch and Torelli 1993). When the questionnaire was subjected to a factor analysis, four factors emerged, which were then divided into two groups: task-related stress and relationship-oriented stress. Koschnick (2002) added another item to the ASI dealing with the disciplining of staff members (verbal or written reprimands, recommendations for suspensions, recommendations for non-renewal of contract, etc.). Koschnick's rationale for the additional item stemmed from the perspective of a principal dealing with collective bargaining issues, whose job entailed more personal attention to disciplining staff. This is an added dimension to the principal's job that was not as prevalent when the original ASI was developed. Dealing with such complicated problems while simultaneously anticipating the bargaining unit's responses makes for a very stressful and difficult situation. Nothing in the literature review alluded to the stressful nature of this dimension of the principal's job. Does a teacher's active participation in the local bargaining unit unduly influence the principal's behavior in disciplining that teacher? It is a relatively new issue and one that could conflict with Indiana's collective bargaining law. For the purposes of this study, the 20-item 1993 version of the ASI was utilized, with the additional item added by Koschnick.

Population. Principals from 239 Indiana high schools encompassing grades 9-12 during the academic year 2002-2003 were surveyed for this study. The added responsibilities of P.L. 221 did not apply to private schools. For this reason, the potential of legislation to add stress to the job of the public high school principal justified limiting the study to public high schools. The names and addresses of the subject pool were drawn from *The Indiana School Directory 2002*.

Of the total number of 239 principals surveyed, 162 (or 67.8 percent) returned the ASI, and 171 (or 71.5 percent) returned the LPI. Demographic data for Indiana's high school principals are shown in Table 1.

Data Analysis. Regarding leadership behavior, this study leads one to conclude that the demographic factors of gender, size of school, or number of years experience as a principal have no statistically significant relationship with patterns of leadership. The patterns of leadership behavior were not different between male and female principals by size of school or by years of experience. Tables 2, 3, and 4 show the mean averages for leadership behaviors by gender, size of school, and length of service.

Of note, the differences in the means between men and women were small to nonexistent in the schools of the largest size. The differences in the means between men and women in the middle-to-smallest schools varied. The largest difference seemed to be between men and women in the smallest schools for the behavior Encouraging the Heart, judged simply by the size of the mean.

As Table 4 illustrates, the study showed no significant differences between gender and length of service as principal; however, in almost all cases, women's

Table 1. Demographic Data on High School Principals in Indiana, 2002-2003, Overall and by Gender (N =162)

Item	All	Men	Women
Average age	50.0	49.7	51.2
Average age when first became principal	40.4	39.4	43.3
Average years of teaching experience	18.3	18.2	18.9
Average years as an assistant principal	5.0	5.0	6.0
Average years as a principal	8.4	8.7	7.2
Average years in current position	5.1	5.0	5.3
Gender		123	39
Number in his/her first year as principal	20	14	6
Number in his/her second year as principal	10	8	2
Number who had served as principal in only one school	78	58	20

self-reported levels of leadership behaviors were higher than those of their male counterparts.

Regression analysis was then used to compare the responses of the principals in relation to the demographic variables under investigation. The demographic variables were compared with the types of leadership tendencies (respondent scores on the subscales of the LPI) with the two types of stress (task or relationship oriented).

The five subscales of the LPI—Challenging the Process, Inspiring a Shared Vision, Enabling Others to Act, Modeling the Way, and Encouraging the Heart—were highly correlated to each other, verifying earlier validation of the internal consistency of the LPI (*alpha* coefficients ranged from .8436 to .6027). The subscales of the LPI were then correlated to the two sources of stress measured by the ASI—Conflict-Mediating or Relationship-Oriented Stress and Task-Oriented Stress (*alpha* coefficients for the two subscales of the ASI were .7727 -.7992). Coefficients emerging from the regression analysis, however, were not statistically significant. (See Table 5.)

The study revealed no dominant patterns of leadership behavior clearly linked to either type of stress. While there were no statistically significant relationships between the subscales of the LPI and conflict-mediating and task-oriented stress, the researchers conducted a more qualitative analysis of the data. A rank-ordered list of the principals' self-assessment of the causes of moderate to significant levels of stress as measured by the ASI was compiled. These data are presented in Table 6. (Items are rank-ordered in all tables, but were ordered differently in the survey.)

Table 2. Mean Averages for Leadership Behaviors by Gender*

Leadership Behavior	Men	Women	All
Challenging the Process (CP)	3.82	3.95	3.85
Inspiring a Shared Vision (ISV)	3.84	3.99	3.88
Enabling Others to Act (EOA)	4.24	4.33	4.26
Modeling the Way (MW)	4.17	4.27	4.23
Encouraging the Heart (EH)	3.94	4.14	3.99

*118 men and 39 women completed the LPI who reported their gender (157 out of a total of 171—14 either did not complete all of the items on the LPI or did not report their gender).

Table 3. Mean Averages for Leadership Behaviors by Size of School and Gender* as Depicted through Subscale of the LPI

	CP		EH		EOA		ISV		MW	
School Size	M	W	W	M	W	M	W	M	W	M
Largest (830-2771)	4.00	3.98	4.04	4.03	4.39	4.21	4.05	4.00	4.29	4.29
Middle (447-829)	3.77	3.86	3.90	4.15	4.15	4.13	4.42	3.80	4.12	4.18
Smallest (82-446)	3.64	3.94	3.90	4.35	4.18	4.41	3.65	3.80	4.15	4.19

*N's as follows: Largest: Men = 44   Women = 16
                  Middle: Men = 39   Women = 14
                  Smallest: Men = 35   Women = 9

Table 4. Mean Averages for Leadership Behaviors by Years of Service and Gender* as Depicted through Subscale of the LPI

	CP		EH		EOA		ISV		MW	
Length of Service	M	W	M	W	M	W	M	W	M	W
<= 6 years	3.77	4.00	3.90	4.09	4.30	4.25	3.85	3.93	4.20	4.27
>= 7 years	3.85	3.89	3.97	4.15	4.25	4.31	3.84	4.03	4.22	4.32

*N's as follows: <=6: Men = 54   Women = 19
                  >=7: Men = 60   Women = 20

Of the leading moderate-to-significant stressors (the nine items cited by 50 percent or more of the principals), two-thirds (six) were in the category of task-oriented stress as opposed to conflict-mediating stress. Furthermore, seven of these stressors might be grouped into the general areas of high volumes of paperwork (1, 6, 7), conflict with teachers (2, 9), and legal issues (1)—issues identified in previous studies as causing major stress on the job. The two remaining items were personal stressors that principals imposed on themselves but nevertheless were inherent in the tasks they were required to perform—having excessively high expectations of themselves and making decisions that affected the lives of others.

Table 5. Correlation Coefficients for the Regression Analysis
of Leadership Behaviors and Types of Stress

Leadership Behavior	Conflict-Mediating Stress	Task-Oriented Stress
Challenging the Process	-.016	.025
Inspiring a Shared Vision	-.001	.020
Enabling Others to Act	-.134	-.130
Modeling the Way	-.008	.017
Encouraging the Heart	.016	.038

Conversely, the two items cited least often as causing moderate to significant stress were those related to students—resolving differences between or among students and handling student discipline problems. This begs the question of whether this could be because the onerous duty is sometimes delegated to assistant principals. Data show 51.3 percent of the principals reported they handled student disciplinary problems only two to five times per week. Fourteen, or 8.1 percent, of the respondents said they delegate the responsibility to someone else.

Of interest, when the stress levels for disciplining students and staff were compared, the results differed dramatically. Approximately 83 percent of the principals indicated they either did not deal with staff conflict (.6 percent) or did so only occasionally (76.7 percent); yet, of the task-oriented items on the ASI, this was the number one stressor reported by principals. Clearly, although the number of disciplinary incidents for both groups was low, the level of stress reported was divergent.

While the demographic data were not significantly different when separated by gender (see Table 1), stress levels in men and women did show some variation. In general, and with only a few exceptions, a higher percentage of women reported moderate to significant levels of stress on the survey items. Table 7 illustrates this.

Eleven items were cited by 50 percent or more of the female principals, while only eight items were cited by 50 percent or more of the male principals. It should be noted, however, that the eight items named by the males were among the 11 cited by the females. One of the three additional items women reported as stressors—working to gain public approval and/or financial support—was ranked ninth by the female principals but 16th by the males. The other two items—resolving differences between/among staff and experiencing pressure for better job performance—were ranked about the same for women and men. The items on the stress inventory were also rank-ordered by size of school. These rankings appear in Table 8.

Administering schools of different size entails dealing with many of the same sources of stress. The sources of stress at the top (items 1 through 3) and bottom (items 18 through 21) remained about the same when compared overall. However, variation in the rankings was observed in those items listed in the middle.

Table 6. Rank Order of Items Indicating Moderate to Significant Levels of Stress Reported in Percentages (N = 162)

Item Rank	Percentage
1. Complying with state, federal, and organizational rules and policies	75.2
2. Disciplining staff members	73.3
3. Imposing excessively high expectations on myself	70.6
4. Making decisions that affect the lives of others	64.4
5. Having too heavy a workload, one that I cannot possibly finish during the normal workday	59.6
6. Completing reports and other paperwork on time	59.6
7. Having school-related meetings take up too much time	59.0
8. Participating in school activities outside normal working hours at the expense of my personal time	58.4
9. Resolving differences between/among staff	50.0
10. Experiencing pressure for better job performance over and above what I think is reasonable	47.2
11. Evaluating staff members' performance	46.9
12. Supervising and coordinating the tasks of many people	44.7
13. Being frequently interrupted by school-related telephone calls	42.2
14. Working to gain public approval and/or financial support	41.6
15. Trying to influence my immediate supervisors' actions and decisions that affect me	39.8
16. Having too much responsibility delegated to me by my supervisor	37.3
17. Resolving parent/school conflicts (head lice, grades, etc.)	37.3
18. Writing memos, letters, and other communications	34.2
19. Having my work interrupted by staff members who want to talk about work-related issues	33.5
20. Resolving differences between/among students	19.4
21. Handling student discipline problems	19.3

In Table 9, items on the stress inventory also were compared by school size and gender.

The data in Table 9 reveal variations in rankings. These differences occurred quite frequently between school size and gender. For example, on the item "Having high expectations for myself," female principals in smaller schools perceived much less stress (rank of nine), while male principals in the smaller schools perceived this as the top-ranked source of stress. In fact, among the top five sources of stress, the rankings varied considerably for males and females. An example of this is the item ranked number five, "Having too heavy a workload." Females (93.8 percent) in small schools ranked this as the number one source of stress, while male respondents (57.8 percent) ranked it number 10, almost a reversal. In medium-sized schools,

Table 7. Rank Order of Items Indicating Moderate to Significant Levels of Stress Reported in Percentages by Gender (N of Men = 123, N of Women = 39)

	Percentages		Ranking	
Item Rank	Men	Women	Men	Women
1. Complying with state, federal, and organizational rules and policies	73.9	97.4	1	1
2. Disciplining staff members	72.3	79.9	2	2
3. Imposing excessively high expectations on myself	67.4	79.4	3	3
4. Making decisions that affect the lives of others	64.2	64.1	4	6
5. Having too heavy a workload, one that I cannot possibly finish during the normal workday	54.4	74.3	8	4
6. Completing reports and other paperwork on time	58.5	61.5	5	7
7. Having school-related meetings take up too much time	55.2	69.2	7	5
8. Participating in school activities outside normal working hours at the expense of my personal time	56.9	61.5	6	8
9. Resolving differences between/among staff	48.7	53.8	9	10
10. Experiencing pressure for better job performance over and above what I think is reasonable	46.3	51.2	11	11
11. Evaluating staff members' performance	48.7	41.0	10	14
12. Supervising and coordinating the tasks of many people	44.7	43.5	12	13
13. Being frequently interrupted by school-related telephone calls	40.6	46.1	13	12
14. Working to gain public approval and/or financial support	36.5	56.4	16	9
15. Trying to influence my immediate supervisors' actions and decisions that affect me	39.0	41.0	15	15
16. Having too much responsibility delegated to me by my supervisor	35.7	41.0	17	16
17. Resolving parent/school conflicts (head lice, grades, etc.)	39.8	28.2	14	17
18. Writing memos, letters, and other communications	35.7	30.7	18	19
19. Having my work interrupted by staff members who want to talk about work-related issues	32.5	35.8	19	18
20. Resolving differences between/among students	21.0	10.2	20	20
21. Handling student discipline problems	19.5	17.9	21	21

female and male principals perceived the top five items almost the same way. In the largest category of schools, some variation can be observed, but not as great as in smaller schools. It should be noted again that the sources listed as least stressful were those dealing with students.

After comparing the principals' responses on school size and gender, the researchers analyzed the data on experience. The items on the ASI were rank-ordered by those

Table 8. Rank Order of Items Indicating Moderate to Significant Levels of Stress by School Size (N = 162)

	School Size		
	830-2771	447-829	82-446
Item Rank	N=58	N=53	N=44
1. Complying with state, federal, and organizational rules and policies	2	1	2
2. Disciplining staff members	1	2	4
3. Imposing excessively high expectations on myself	3	3	1
4. Making decisions that affect the lives of others	4	7	3
5. Having too heavy a workload, one that I cannot possibly finish during the normal workday	8	4	8
6. Completing reports and other paperwork on time	5	8	5
7. Having school-related meetings take up too much time	6	6	7
8. Participating in school activities outside normal working hours at the expense of my personal time	9	5	6
9. Resolving differences between/among staff	7	11	13
10. Experiencing pressure for better job performance over and above what I think is reasonable	12	9	10
11. Evaluating staff members' performance	11	16	9
12. Supervising and coordinating the tasks of many people	14	10	15
13. Being frequently interrupted by school-related telephone calls	10	17	12
14. Working to gain public approval and/or financial support	13	12	19
15. Trying to influence my immediate supervisors' actions and decisions that affect me	15	13	11
16. Having too much responsibility delegated to me by my supervisor	18	15	14
17. Resolving parent/school conflicts (head lice, grades, etc.)	19	14	18
18. Writing memos, letters, and other communications	17	18	17
19. Having my work interrupted by staff members who want to talk about work-related issues	16	19	16
20. Resolving differences between/among students	21	20	20
21. Handling student discipline problems	20	21	21

principals who had six or fewer years of experience and by those who had more than six years of experience. The comparison of those rankings is presented in table 10.

The data in Table 10 reveal a few variations in rankings between the two groups. Overall, experience as a principal did not prove to be a discriminating variable. The more experienced group ranked some of the items as more stressful than their younger counterparts, but the reverse was also true.

Table 9. Rank Order of Items Indicating Moderate to Significant Levels of Stress by School Size and Gender (N = 162)

Item Rank	School Size					
	830-2771		447-829		82-446	
	M	F	M	F	M	F
1. Complying with state, federal, and organizational rules and policies	2	3	1	1	2	2
2. Disciplining staff members	1	2	2	5	5	6
3. Imposing excessively high expectations on myself	5	1	3	2	1	9
4. Making decisions that affect the lives of others	3	8	7	8	3	5
5. Having too heavy a workload, one that I cannot possibly finish during the normal workday	6	7	4	4	10	1
6. Completing reports and other paperwork on time	4	6	8	6	4	8
7. Having school-related meetings take up too much time	7	4	6	3	7	7
8. Participating in school activities outside normal working hours at the expense of my personal time	8	9	5	10	8	3
9. Resolving differences between/among staff	10	5	11	17	13	17
10. Experiencing pressure for better job performance over and above what I think is reasonable	14	10	9	9	9	11
11. Evaluating staff members' performance	9	15	17	11	6	16
12. Supervising and coordinating the tasks of many people	12	13	10	13	16	18
13. Being frequently interrupted by school-related telephone calls	11	12	19	7	12	13
14. Working to gain public approval and/or financial support	13	11	14	12	19	4
15. Trying to influence my immediate supervisors' actions and decisions that affect me	16	14	13	14	11	12
16. Having too much responsibility delegated to me by my supervisor	18	18	16	16	18	10
17. Resolving parent/school conflicts (head lice, grades, etc.)	19	19	12	18	14	19
18. Writing memos, letters, and other communications	17	17	15	19	17	15
19. Having my work interrupted by staff members who want to talk about work-related issues	15	16	21	15	15	14
20. Resolving differences between/among students	21	21	18	21	20	20
21. Handling student discipline problems	20	20	20	20	21	21

While the data regarding experience as a principal showed few variations in rankings, experience and gender were compared to complete the analysis. These data are shown in Table 11.

Among the top eight sources of stress, "Disciplining staff members" was reported as being more stressful by the less experienced male principals than their female counterparts, while "School meetings that take up too much time" was reported as

Table 10. Rank Order of Items Indicating Moderate to Significant Levels of Stress Reported in Percentages by Years of Experience in Principalship (N = 162)

Item Rank	yrs. of exp.	Percentages		Ranking	
		<=6	>=7	<=6	>=7
1. Complying with state, federal, and organizational rules and policies		70.2	80.4	2	1
2. Disciplining staff members		77.0	70.7	1	3
3. Imposing excessively high expectations on myself		70.2	70.7	3	2
4. Making decisions that affect the lives of others		64.8	63.4	4	6
5. Having too heavy a workload, one that I cannot possibly finish during the normal workday		59.4	58.5	5	8
6. Completing reports and other paperwork on time		54.0	63.4	8	5
7. Having school-related meetings take up too much time		55.5	62.2	7	7
8. Participating in school activities outside normal working hours at the expense of my personal time		50.0	67.0	9	4
9. Resolving differences between/among staff		56.7	43.9	6	13
10. Experiencing pressure for better job performance over and above what I think is reasonable		43.2	54.8	12	9
11. Evaluating staff members' performance		43.2	50.0	13	10
12. Supervising and coordinating the tasks of many people		47.2	41.4	10	14
13. Being frequently interrupted by school-related telephone calls		41.8	43.9	14	12
14. Working to gain public approval and/or financial support		44.5	40.2	11	15
15. Trying to influence my immediate supervisors' actions and decisions that affect me		36.4	43.9	15	11
16. Having too much responsibility delegated to me by my supervisor		35.1	39.0	16	16
17. Resolving parent/school conflicts (head lice, grades, etc.)		35.1	39.0	17	17
18. Writing memos, letters, and other communications		32.4	37.8	19	18
19. Having my work interrupted by staff members who want to talk about work-related issues		33.7	32.9	18	19
20. Resolving differences between/among students		17.5	20.7	20	21
21. Handling student discipline problems		16.2	23.1	21	20

more stressful by the female principals than their male counterparts. There was little variation in the rankings of the more experienced group regardless of gender.

When school size and years of experience as a principal were compared, variation in the rankings was commonplace. These rankings are presented in Table 12.

Gender was not used as a variable in Table 12 because of small numbers in the groups. The reader might want to look at the differences in the rankings in Table 12. For example, the variation in disciplining staff members was reported less often

Table 11. Rank Order of Items Indicating Moderate to Significant Levels of Stress by Gender and Years of Experience in Principalship
(Overall N = 162; N of <=6 yrs. =73; N of >=7 yrs. = 89)

		Ranking			
	yrs. of exp.	<=6 yrs		>=7 yrs	
Item Rank		M	F	M	F
1. Complying with state, federal, and organizational rules and policies		2	3	1	1
2. Disciplining staff members		1	5	3	2
3. Imposing excessively high expectations on myself		3	1	2	3
4. Making decisions that affect the lives of others		4	6	6	7
5. Having too heavy a workload, one that I cannot possibly finish during the normal workday		6	4	8	5
6. Completing reports and other paperwork on time		7	7	5	8
7. Having school-related meetings take up too much time		9	2	7	6
8. Participating in school activities outside normal working hours at the expense of my personal time		8	10	4	4
9. Resolving differences between/among staff		5	8	16	11
10. Experiencing pressure for better job performance over and above what I think is reasonable		12	12	9	9
11. Evaluating staff members' performance		10	17	10	13
12. Supervising and coordinating the tasks of many people		11	9	11	18
13. Being frequently interrupted by school-related telephone calls		14	13	13	12
14. Working to gain public approval and/or financial support		13	11	19	10
15. Trying to influence my immediate supervisors' actions and decisions that affect me		16	16	12	14
16. °Having too much responsibility delegated to me by my supervisor		18	15	14	16
17. Resolving parent/school conflicts (head lice, grades, etc.)		15	19	15	17
18. Writing memos, letters, and other communications		17	18	17	15
19. Having my work interrupted by staff members who want to talk about work-related issues		19	14	18	21
20. Resolving differences between/among students		20	20	20	20
21. Handling student discipline problems		21	21	21	19

as stressful by the more experienced group of principals in the smaller schools. Completing reports and other paperwork was reported as more stressful by the less experienced group of principals in the middle-sized schools. In the larger schools, the less experienced principals reported "Having too heavy a workload" as more stressful than their more experienced counterparts. Although ranked at a lower level of stress, "Resolving differences between/among staff" was reported quite differently by principals in the middle- and smaller-sized schools.

Table 12. Rank Order of Items Indicating Moderate to Significant Levels of Stress by School Size and Years of Experience (N = 162)

| | | School Size | | | | | |
| | | 830-2771 | | 447-829 | | 82-446 | |
Item Rank	yrs. of exp.	<=6	>=7	<=6	>=7	<=6	>=7
1. Complying with state, federal, and organizational rules and policies		2	2	2	1	4	1
2. Disciplining staff members		1	1	1	2	3	8
3. Imposing excessively high expectations on myself		3	3	3	3	1	2
4. Making decisions that affect the lives of others		5	4	8	9	2	5
5. Having too heavy a workload, one that I cannot possibly finish during the normal workday		4	10	4	5	6	9
6. Completing reports and other paperwork on time		6	6	14	6	5	6
7. Having school-related meetings take up too much time		7	7	5	7	11	4
8. Participating in school activities outside normal working hours at the expense of my personal time		10	5	7	4	8	3
9. Resolving differences between/among staff		8	8	9	15	7	18
10. Experiencing pressure for better job performance over and above what I think is reasonable		12	12	15	8	12	10
11. Evaluating staff members' performance		15	9	13	18	9	7
12. Supervising and coordinating the tasks of many people		13	14	6	10	13	16
13. Being frequently interrupted by school-related telephone calls		9	13	16	16	16	11
14. Working to gain public approval and/or financial support		14	11	10	12	10	19
15. Trying to influence my immediate supervisors' actions and decisions that affect me		16	15	17	11	14	13
16. Having too much responsibility delegated to me by my supervisor		17	18	12	17	18	12
17. Resolving parent/school conflicts (head lice, grades, etc.)		18	17	11	13	17	15
18. Writing memos, letters, and other communications		19	16	18	14	15	17
19. Having my work interrupted by staff members who want to talk about work-related issues		11	19	19	20	19	14
20. Resolving differences between/among students		21	21	20	21	20	20
21. Handling student discipline problems		20	20	21	19	21	21

Summary and Discussion

The statistical analysis conducted in this study confirmed the LPI and the ASI as valid instruments for collecting data on leadership behavior and administrator stress. High *alpha* correlation coefficients were derived for each of the subscales of the LPI and the two dimensions of administrator stress, thereby suggesting high internal consistency. No dominant patterns of leadership behaviors were highly correlated with either type of stress that was measured by the ASI.

No statistically significant correlations were found between leadership behaviors and the two types of stress. When a qualitative approach was used in analyzing the data, however, important findings emerged that might be applied in schools. The principals consistently reported disciplining staff members and complying with federal and state regulations as moderate to significant sources of stress. This was true for male principals as well as females and remained constant regardless of school size and experience level of the principal.

Another consistent finding that cut across all three demographic variables was the principals' view of student discipline as a lesser source of stress. Taking into account all of the demographic variables under investigation, in all of the analyses, the principals consistently viewed dealing with students and their problems as lesser sources of stress. This might be partially explained by the principals delegating student discipline problems to subordinates, because the principals reported dealing with student discipline problems only two to five times per week. It could also be that the principals viewed student discipline and student problems as expected parts of their job. On the other hand, the principals reported dealing with disciplining staff members only occasionally, yet they viewed it as a major source of stress when it *did* occur (76.7 percent reported that they dealt with staff conflict only occasionally, while .6 percent reported not dealing with staff conflict at all).

In investigating gender as a variable, female principals reported moderate to significant stress more often than their male counterparts. Fifty percent of the female respondents listed 11 items on the stress index as sources of stress, while the male respondents listed only eight. The eight items the male respondents listed were included within the 11 the females listed. Do women report more stress because they feel compelled to continue working harder to maintain their positions of leadership? We simply do not know.

The female respondents had higher average scores on the LPI than did their male counterparts. This raises other interesting issues concerning gender. Do women feel that if they have risen to the level of principal leadership they have had to overcome more barriers than men and therefore have more self-confidence? There is a common perception that leadership differences exist between males and females. This study, however, would lead one to conclude that self-reported leadership behaviors do not vary by gender. Any differences may stem from observed behavior rather than individuals' perceptions of their own behavior. We postulate that leadership is leadership, and the gender issue may simply complicate the concept. This conclusion is in keeping with the previous research of Brunner (1999) and Ortiz and Marshall (1988).

Investigating gender and size of school, we found that in average-sized (447-829 student enrollment) high schools in Indiana there were differences in the sources of stress for the male and female respondents. For example, 93.8 percent of the female respondents reported "Imposing excessively high expectations on myself," while only 57.8 percent of the male respondents reported this as a source of stress. On the other hand, the item "Too much responsibility delegated to me by my superior" was ranked by 53.3 percent of the males, while only 37.5 percent of the females reported it as a source of stress. In larger high schools, more items were reported as stressors by females, and the items differed between sizes of schools.

While there were differences between experienced principals and their sources of stress as compared with their lesser-experienced colleagues, overall the differences were negligible. When the data were compared by size of school and experience level of the principals, the rankings differed noticeably. Johnson's earlier research (2002) indicated both experienced and less-experienced principals recognized unreasonable standards and pressures of accountability as sources of stress. The same proved true in this study.

Confirming Koschnick's conclusion (2002), an overwhelming majority of the respondents cited disciplining staff members as a major source of stress. In states where collective bargaining is heavily practiced, this might be a crisis situation for the principal when his or her actions in dealing with staff conflict run afoul of bargaining agreements. (Does a principal discipline staff or faculty who are members of the local bargaining unit?) This study supports earlier research pointing to long working hours, high volumes of paperwork, and conflict with teachers as sources of stress found by Gmelch 1978, Hanson 1996, Cedoline 1982, and Gmelch and Torelli 1993. No link, however, was found to disciplining a staff or faculty member who was affiliated with the bargaining unit.

Several major conclusions can be drawn from this study. Leadership behavior was assessed by a reputable instrument, the LPI, and the data analysis revealed no significant differences in dominant patterns of leadership between male and female respondents. We, therefore, conclude that gender as a discerning variable in the study of leadership behavior, at least among the participants in this study, had no predictive value. Because no clearly dominant patterns of leadership emerged from the participants, we conclude that no discernible leadership behavior is more stress prone than another, as far as the subscales of the LPI depict leader behavior. We also assert that no clear linkage exists between the leadership behavior of principals in large, middle-sized, and small schools and the two sources of stress. The same holds true for principal experience and stress.

References

Bales, R.F. (1953). *Interaction process analysis*. Cambridge, MA: Addison-Wesley.

Banach, W. (2001). *The top ten educational hot/nots*. Paper presented at the Indiana Association of Public School Superintendents Conference, Indianapolis, IN.

Blake, R.R., & Mouton, J.S. (1994). *The managerial grid: Leadership styles for achieving production through people*. Houston, TX: Gulf Publishing.

Brimm, J. (1983). What stresses school administrators. *Theory Into Practice, 22*(1), 65-69.

Brock, B.L., & Grady, M.L. (2002). *Avoiding burnout: A principal's guide to keeping the fire alive*. Thousand Oaks, CA: Corwin Press.

Brunner, C.C. (1999). *Sacred dreams: Women and the superintendency*. Albany, NY: State University of New York.

Burns, J.M. (1978). *Leadership*. New York: Harper and Row.

Cedoline, A. (1982). *Job burnout in public education: Symptoms, causes, and survival skills*. New York: Teachers College Press.

Edmonds, R. (1979). Effective schools for the urban poor. *Educational Leadership, 37*, 15-27.

Educational Research Service. (1998). *Is there a shortage of qualified candidates for openings in the principalship? An exploratory study*. Alexandria, VA: National Association of Elementary School Principals and Reston, VA: National Association of Secondary School Principals.

Fiedler, F.E. (1967). *A theory of leadership effectiveness*. New York: McGraw-Hill.

Gmelch, W. (1978). The principal's next challenge: The twentieth century art of managing stress. *NASSP Bulletin, 62*(415), 5-12.

Gmelch, W., & Torelli, J. (1993). *People and Education, 1*(4), 363-381.

Halpin, A., & Winer, B. (1957). A factorial study of the leader behavior descriptions. In R. Stogdill & A. Coons (Eds.), *Leader behavior: Its description and measurement* (pp. 39-51). Columbus, OH: Ohio State University, Bureau of Business Research, Monograph 88.

Hanson, M. (1996). *Educational administration and organizational behavior* (4th ed.). Needham Heights, MA: Simon and Schuster.

Hersey P., & Blanchard, K. (1982). *Management of organizational behavior* (4th ed.). Englewood Cliffs, NJ: Prentice-Hall.

Indiana Department of Education. (2002). *The Indiana school directory*. Indianapolis, IN: Indiana Department of Education, Division of Publications.

Institute of Educational Leadership. (2000). *Leadership for student learning: Reinventing the principalship*. Washington, DC: Author.

Johnson, J. (2002). Staying ahead of the game. *Educational Leadership, 59*(8), 26-29.

Koschnick, J. (2002). *The relationship between leadership style and administrative stress*. Unpublished doctoral dissertation, Ball State University, Muncie, IN.

Kouzes, J.M., & Posner, B.Z. (1993). *Credibility: How leaders gain and lose it, why people demand it*. San Francisco: Jossey-Bass.

Kowalski, T.J. (1999). *The school superintendent: Theory, practice, and cases*. Columbus, OH: Prentice Hall.

Lunenburg, F., & Ornstein, A. (2000). *Educational administration* (3rd ed.). Belmont, CA: Wadsworth/Thomas.

Malone, B., Sharp, W., & Thompson, J. (2000). *The Indiana principalship: Perception of principals, aspiring principals, and the superintendents*. Paper presented at the Midwest Educational Research Association Conference, Chicago.

McGregor, D. (1960). *The human side of enterprise*. New York: McGraw-Hill.

Milstein, M., & Farkas, J. (1988). The over-stated case of educator stress. *The Journal of Educational Administration, 26*, 4.

Ogawa, R., & Bossert S. (1995). Leadership as an organizational quality. *Educational Administration Quarterly, 31*(2), 224-243.

Ortiz, F.I., & Marshall, C. (1988). Women in educational administration. In N. Boyan (Ed.), *Handbook of research on educational administration* (pp. 123-141). New York: Longman.

Sergiovanni, T.J., & Elliott, D. (1975). *Educational and organizational leadership in elementary schools.* Englewood Cliffs, NJ: Prentice-Hall.

Sternberg, R.E. (2000). Acts of aggression. *The School Administrator, 57*(10), 6-15.

Stogdill, R.M. (1974). *Handbook of leadership: A survey of theory and research.* New York: The Free Press.

Tallerico, M. (1999). Women and the superintendency: What do we really know? In C. Brunner (Ed.), *Sacred dreams: Women and the superintendency* (pp. 29-48). Albany, NY: State University of New York Press.

Ubben, G.C., & Hughes, L.W. (1997). *The principal: Creative leadership for effective schools* (3rd ed.). Needham Heights, MA: Allyn and Bacon.

Wesson, L.H., & Grady, M.L. (1994). An analysis of women urban superintendents: A national study. *Urban Education, 28*(4), 412-424.

Yackel, I. (1984). *An analysis of leadership styles and stress in the rural principalship.* Regina, Saskatchewan: The Research Center, Saskatchewan School Trustees Association (ERIC Document Reproduction Service No. ED260511).

Bobby G. Malone is a professor in the Department of Educational Leadership, and Jacquelyn S. Nelson is assistant dean of the Graduate School, both at Ball State University.

Chapter 8: Questions for Reflection and Discussion

1. In this study, the researchers use a qualitative survey to determine administrator stressors. What do you consider items of moderate to significant levels of stress?

2. How would you rank the order of the stressors identified in Tables 6-12? Are your rankings consistent with the survey findings?

3. Principals viewed disciplining staff members as a source of significant stress, despite reporting that the majority rarely dealt with staff discipline. Do you consider disciplining staff members a significant stressor? What techniques do you use when disciplining staff? Is this an area in which you feel more training would be helpful?

4. The authors discuss some of the causes and possible effects of administrator stress. How has the stress level affected you? Are you concerned about experiencing "leader burnout"? Do you have any suggestions for other administrators on how to handle stress?

9

System Versus Personnel Leadership: Finding the Right Leader for Your School

Daniel J. Keenan

It's crunch time, and the pressure is on. You need a coach to step up and lead the team to victory. Does your leader's course of action vary depending on the field, the weather, or the opponent?

Like football, education is always experiencing a "crunch time," and circumstances vary greatly from one "play" to the next. Finding the right leader to run a school is as essential to its success as finding the perfect coach to lead a team to victory.

In this article, author Daniel J. Keenan relates his observations of successful leaders to conclude that successful leaders can be divided into the categories of "system" leaders and "personnel" leaders.

What are the factors that help determine who will lead well in particular environments? Can the same leadership style be effective in an urban school and a suburban school, a small school and a large school? How about in a high-achieving school and a struggling school, or an ethnically homogenous school and a culturally diverse school? Does the environment determine the type of leader needed, or does a great leader create his or her environment?

Based on my experiences in several school districts, I have concluded that successful leaders can be categorized as one of two types of leaders: "system" leaders, who enforce a specific, effective system to succeed, and "personnel" leaders, who build a system around the strengths of the people involved.

The System Leader

System leaders typically subscribe to a methodical way to achieve and sustain success, and focus on instilling their processes and plans to create that success. They have faith that their system is the best way to lead schools to higher achievement.

System leaders can perhaps be the most effective leaders of all, but they must find—or create—a culture that subscribes to their system.

Every culture can accept a style that seems contradictory to what it has accepted in the past. This is usually the case when a great change is needed or an organization has reached desperate times. In either case, the seemingly contradictory style may prove successful, but any sustained success requires a commitment to the new culture, even during tough times.

Examples of System Leaders

As an exemplary system leader, National Football League coach Bill Parcells has had great success in different environments. During his tenure, Parcells took over three losing football teams and turned them into championship teams. In each environment, however, he created the same culture and was able to move the organization forward within that culture. Parcells' success was predicated on the assurance that his direct and assertive leadership style was understood throughout the organization and that the people he surrounded himself with were the type of followers that best fit his assertive style. He has proven time after time that he can bring success to an organization when he is given full control of its operations. Without this control, Parcells' leadership style is just another of many that may work if it clicks with the right people, in the right place, at the right time.

In my first teaching experience, which was in a small rural district in Indiana, the principal ran a tight ship and excelled at leading the school. His rugged, no-nonsense personality matched the culture of the community and the school. Most of the teachers grew up in the same region and adhered to his values, and he related to the students and the community with little conflict. Rules for students and staff were clear-cut and were followed strictly and consistently. Zero tolerance was embraced by the community and enforced by district administration. A traditional top-down authority structure was in place, and a respect for the "chain of command" was instilled in not only the staff but also with the students and the community.

I often thought about his style and how he achieved such effective results. It became clear that his manner and personality were a good fit for a school in this environment. I think he would agree that he would likely struggle in an urban district, mainly because he would feel uncomfortable, or like a fish out of water. His success depended on his system that was based on values common to a small rural district.

While working in an urban district in Ohio that went through a great demographic change, I saw firsthand how a great leader in one environment is not deemed as effective in another. The principal for years was regarded as an above-average administrator who made sound decisions and led his school to considerable achievement. The staff was willing to go the extra mile to follow his lead.

Then the transient district went through many changes in an eight-year span, and the principal witnessed consistently lower academic results and dwindling student, and consequently staff, morale. Staff members began to look for support and assistance only to find that their frustrations over adjusting to the change were shared by the principal. When the time came to replace him, the school was careful to find a candidate who matched the school's need for different leadership.

It was clear that the former principal was a great system leader whose environment had changed. The change in culture of the school required a change in the systematic processes necessary for success. The new principal addressed the needs of the students by making several system changes immediately. For example, she surveyed the students as to why student activity was so slow. In response to their answers, she eliminated the traditional flag corps (consisting of three members) that accompanied the band and added a step/dance team that had more than 40 student members the first year. She also put into place several tutoring programs in conjunction with local churches, supported initially by certified staff, to help struggling students. By making these and other changes, the new principal demonstrated success with student, and consequently staff, morale.

Finally, Joe Clark, the famous school leader who inspired the movie *Lean On Me,* is another example of a notable system leader. His system, highly structured and based on zero tolerance, was contrary to that of the culture in which he was placed at Paterson, N.J.'s Eastside High School. On a single day during his first week at the school, Clark expelled 300 students for fighting, vandalism, drug possession, profanity, or abusing teachers. After two years, New Jersey's governor declared the school, formerly considered reprehensible, to be a model school, and Clark was named one of the nation's 10 "Principals of Leadership" in 1986.

Only with the school's support through tough times did Clark succeed in molding the culture to one that valued his system. Clark likely would argue that he could work in any environment given the appropriate authority to do things his way.

Just like Parcells, Clark has demonstrated that widespread belief and support in a well-thought-out system can reap positive results. However, a community must be willing to change, and often a need for change must be established for this to occur. It is less likely that Joe Clark or Bill Parcells could easily convert a culture already seeing success to one compatible with their leadership style.

The Personnel Leader

The second type of leader is one who possesses the same essential characteristics as the system leader, yet is very comfortable with change and diverse environments. Known as personnel leaders, these leaders look at the needs of the culture they are involved in and build programs around that culture to reach a high level of achievement. Such leaders not only recognize the strengths of their colleagues, but also continually seek paths toward the improvement of all personnel.

Examples of Personnel Leaders

While working for a suburban school district in Indiana, I taught under a principal who constantly adapted programs to address the school's diversity of students. Change was a positive word, and the principal required educators to team up to engage in action research to improve the school. Teachers were encouraged to use the resources of a nearby university and to collaborate with other professionals to find ways to improve. As a good example of a personnel leader, the principal ensured that the curricular programs put in place accommodated students' needs.

Another personnel leader I taught under surveyed staff, students, and the community to arrive at a plan for a two-year transition to a block schedule. The principal used the strengths of various teacher-leaders to create a pilot program, and he extended professional development once the schedule was fully implemented. He made sure that the timeline for the program's implementation mirrored the progress of his staff, and that adjustments were made to the schedule based on input from stakeholders. By working to understand the needs of this school community, the principal created an environment where student achievement improved.

One might argue that system leaders and personnel leaders have the same result in mind and that there are many examples of both types of leaders who have achieved success. I would argue that the personnel leader would likely make the easiest transition from one type of district or building to the next, but that a system leader who gained the support and time from the community could achieve equal, if not greater, success. The right person for a position of leadership is highly dependent on the needs of the culture.

Similar Theories of Leadership

The two types of leaders described, system leaders and personnel leaders, in many ways tie in with Robert House's path-goal theory of leadership (Northhouse, 2001). House describes that the basic idea behind his path-goal theory is that the leader helps to define goals, clarify the path, remove obstacles, and provide support. In this theory, House perceives how a task-oriented leader, similar to a system leader, is most effective in an environment where the work force is performing unstructured jobs. This leader provides structure. In contrast, a leader who focuses on relationships works best in an environment where the work force is already performing highly structured jobs, which is similar to a personnel leader.

An educational setting focusing on measurable results is more task-oriented. In the case where the school mission or vision is tied to goals that are not data-measurable, the environment is unstructured, as is the case where a results-oriented goal is set, but the curriculum is not clearly aligned with the goal. The first case results in a need for a clear goal; the second requires a clear path.

It is important to note that a personnel leader can still work well in an environment where unstructured jobs are being performed as long as he or she recognizes the strengths of the workers and provides guidance. Likewise, a system leader can work with employees performing highly structured tasks, so long as they fit the leader's system.

The personnel leader's style can also be very closely aligned to that of the "situational" leader described by Hersey and Blanchard (1982). This type of leader matches his or her style to the situation depending on the personnel performing the task. The system leader, on the other hand, is more similar to one described in Fiedler and Garcia's "contingency" theory. This theory is often referred to as "leader-match" because it proposes that effective leadership is contingent on matching a leader's style to the right setting (Northhouse, 2001).

Which Leader Is Right for Your School?

As more of an expert on successful processes, a system leader would fit very well if a school's vision or mission has already been established and the school simply requires a specific system to be run well. This is often the case in rural schools that have a homogenous culture and shared values.

This type of leader sometimes succeeds in suburban buildings where the process has been established and the torch needs only to be passed on from the previous leader. In an urban setting, a system leader may see success if the mission or vision has been established, the leader is a "fit," and the staff and students are not very transient or if a new staff is brought in specifically with the mission or vision in mind. Finally, with strong central-office support, this type of leader may thrive in a school where the staff and students are so frustrated by a lack of achievement that they are seeking a drastic change or system to help.

A personnel leader, more of an expert on people, would likely adapt to any of the above situations and find initial success more quickly—but he or she may need time to get the right system working so that long-term results in achievement can be maximized.

Conclusion

Who do you choose to take you across the goal line when it's fourth and one and time is running out?

The system leader is going to call the bread-and-butter play based on what he or she has researched will work in these situations. If the play results in a touchdown, confidence in the system will grow and so will the team. If not, the system leader will look at the film and determine what wasn't executed properly, but remain with the system.

The personnel leader is going to look at how the current team functions and call a play that best fits the players on the roster to win the game and build on that success. If the play is not successful, he or she will reassess the players and conditions and research how to best use the current resources to make the play the next time.

A team needs a leader to step up and lead the team to victory. It's time for you to make the call for your school, because the clock is ticking, the crowd is anxious, and the game is on the line.

References

Hersey, P., & Blanchard, K. (1982). *Management of organizational behavior: Utilizing human resources.* Englewood Cliffs, NJ: Prentice Hall.

Northhouse, P. (2001). *Leadership theory and practice, 2nd edition.* Thousand Oaks, CA: Sage Publications.

Related Resources

Covey, S. (1990). *Principle-centered leadership.* New York: Fireside.

Kanugo, R., & Mendonca, M. (1996). *Ethical dimensions of leader*ship. Thousand Oaks, CA: Sage Publications.

Kouzes, J., & Posner, B. (1995). *The leadership challenge: How to keep getting extraordinary things done in organizations.* San Francisco: Jossey Bass.

Rost, J. (1991). *Leadership for the 21st century.* New York: Praeger Publications.

Senge, P. (1990). *The fifth discipline: The art and practice of the learning organization.* New York: Doubleday.

Daniel J. Keenan is assistant superintendent of Kenston Local Schools, Chagrin Falls, Ohio.

Chapter 9: Questions for Reflection and Discussion

1. The author describes two types of leaders—system leaders and personnel leaders. Which type best describes your leadership style? The leadership style of others in your district?

2. Bill Parcels and Joe Clark are mentioned as archetypical leaders. Who are your leadership role models? Would you characterize them to be system or personnel leaders?

3. Successful environments for each leader type are discussed in this chapter, with a description of both ideal and challenging environments for each type. Based on your experience and observations, to what extent do you agree or disagree with these characterizations?

4. If you were asked to fill the leadership positions in your district, which leadership style would you want for each position?

10 Careers of School Leaders: What State and District Policy Makers Need to Know

Susan M. Gates, Jeanne S. Ringel, Lucrecia Santibañez, and

Abigail Brown

There is concern that now, as state and federal governments are increasing school accountability requirements and relying on school administrators to promote improvement, schools and districts will not be able to attract and retain enough qualified people to fill these positions. This report develops a conceptual structure for understanding the careers of schools administrators and describes what is known about those who hold such positions and how their characteristics have changed over time. It also describes how factors such as wages, working conditions, entry barriers, and incentives influence individuals' decisions to seek particular administrative positions.

Based on their review and analysis of existing research and empirical data, the authors find there is little evidence of a nationwide crisis in the labor market for school administrators. They do, however, identify three key areas of concern: substantial variation in financial rewards at the state and local levels, barriers to entry into the field that affect people's willingness to become administrators, and an administrative population with many members nearing retirement.

In recent years, policy makers and the public at large have increasingly worried that there is—or soon will be—a shortage of qualified individuals to fill formal management positions in our nation's schools (Colvin 2000). These concerns have several important and distinct dimensions:

- A large number of people are leaving school administration positions.

- Districts have a hard time finding people to replace those who leave.

- Those replacements often lack the skills required to succeed in school administration positions.

Policy makers at the national, state, and local levels have been working to address the recruiting and retention challenges in various ways. Nationally, the Council of Chief State School Officers has emphasized quality and preparation issues. At the state level, there are calls to change administrative certification requirements in hopes of attracting new people into the field (e.g., by offering an "alternative route to certification" for those with non-educational career backgrounds). Some states also are trying to improve the quality of training that principals receive or to make it easier for people to acquire the training. At the local level, many districts—particularly large urban districts—are trying to facilitate recruiting by increasing the supply of people interested in and qualified for school administration positions through mentoring programs for prospective administrators (Colvin 2000) or district-sponsored administrative preparation programs. In addition, some districts have increased administrative salaries, often in targeted ways.

While efforts at all levels appear to be reasonable, each option suggests a different understanding of the underlying cause of the challenges facing schools and districts in terms of recruiting and retaining school administrators. Some responses suggest that low pay is a key issue, others that working conditions are problematic, and still others suggest that certification is a barrier to recruitment.

An empirically-based understanding of the career patterns of school administrators, the moves they make, and the factors that might be expected to influence those moves can help us understand the supply side of the labor market for school administrators. This can help us begin to answer the question of whether the nation is facing a crisis in recruitment and retention, specify the potential causes of such a crisis if it exists, and contribute to the overall policy debate.

A recent study by the RAND Corporation (Gates et al. 2003) provides a detailed empirical baseline against which it is possible to consider current claims of challenges in recruiting and retaining school administrators and to evaluate potential solutions. This paper summarizes some of the key findings of that report.

The study addressed three key questions about the careers of school administrators:

- What are the characteristics of school administrators and how have they changed over time?

- What kinds of movement are taking place into and out of the administrative career field and what factors are likely to affect these entry and exit decisions?

- What kinds of movement are taking place between different types of positions within the administrative career path?

- What kinds of movement are taking place within the principalship, and what does the evidence reveal about the relationship between position turnover and school characteristics?

The report develops a conceptual framework for understanding the careers of school administrators, and uses that framework to address the questions articulated above. The analysis draws on a broad review of the existing literature as well as analyses of career-related issues such as salary, career paths, and attitudes using the Schools and Staffing Survey (SASS) data from the Department of Education, and the Current Population Survey (CPS) from the U.S. Census Bureau.

In this article, we present some descriptive information on school administrators and summarize some of the key conclusions from the paper's analytic results. We begin by presenting the framework for understanding the careers of school administrators.

Understanding Career Flow of School Administrators

Figure 1 describes our conceptualization of career flow for school administrators. The administrative career field includes not only the principalship and the superintendency, but other administrative positions at both the school and district levels, such as assistant principal, business manager, and public affairs specialist. We use this figure to structure our discussion of what we know about the careers of school administrators.

Movement into or out of the administrative career field reflects an individual's decision to enter or leave any position within that field. The career field boundary distinction draws a line between positions in that career field and other activities, which can include teaching, retirement, unemployment, or employment in another industry or organization outside of the career field.

Public policy makers may want to examine whether public school administrators are leaving their jobs and seeking similar positions in private schools. In order to address this question, they would want to define the career field in terms of public school administration only, and treat moves from the public to the private sector as movement out of the career field. Similarly, policy makers may be interested in the extent to which individuals are crossing state or district lines even within the public sector. To examine these issues, it would be necessary to think of the career field in terms of the state or the district.

In our research, we use this definition of education administration career field to summarize what we currently know about school administrators and their careers.

We begin with a description of the characteristics of current administrators (the boxes) and how those characteristics changed over time, and then examine the moves that individuals make in the context of an administrative career (the arrows). We segment our discussion of the moves administrators make into two parts: moves into and out of the school administration career field, and finally, moves within the principalship. Movement into and out of the administrative career field may be related to how attractive school administration is relative to teaching, positions outside of education or leisure/retirement. Examination of this topic helps inform the question of whether school administrators are being lured away from careers in education by more attractive outside alternatives, and whether teachers have the incentive to move into administration. Movement within the principalship may be influenced by the relative attractiveness of different jobs. Examination of this topic allows us to consider whether some schools are at an advantage or disadvantage in attracting and retaining principals and whether there may a "crisis" for particular types of schools, even if there is no evidence of a nationwide crisis.

In our report, we examine two types of evidence related to the moves individuals make: evidence on the moves themselves and factors that might be expected to influence those moves.

Overview of Current School Administrators

Figure 2 summarizes what we know about the number of people who fill each box in the administrative career paths in both the private and the public sectors. It is clear from the figure that school administrators are a small group compared with teachers. The number of principals is only 2.5 percent of the number of teachers in public schools and 6 percent in private schools. The number of all administrators (principals, superintendents, and other administrators) is 6.5 percent of the number of teachers in public schools and 12 percent in private schools.

In 1999-2000, there were about 110,000 principals, 76 percent of whom worked in public schools, as shown in table 1. School administration was not a rapidly grow-ing career field in the late 1980s and 1990s. Between 1987-88 and 1999-2000, the number of principals grew by more than 7 percent for public schools and by more than 3 percent for private schools. However, these national averages obscure sub-stantial regional and sectoral differences. In the public sector, there was growth in each region, but growth was substantially higher in the West than in other regions. The private sector saw declines in the number of principals in the Northeast and Midwest, and increases in the South and West.

In the 1999-2000 school year, there were 988 charter school principals, and their characteristics differed markedly from those of all public school principals, as reflected in Table 2.

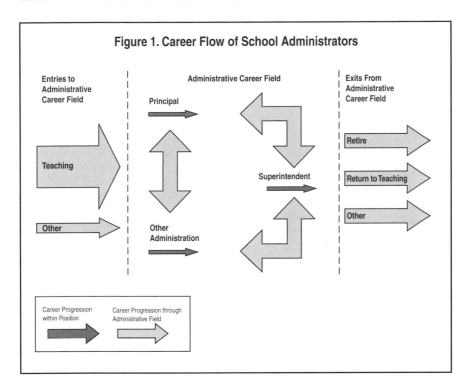

Figure 1. Career Flow of School Administrators

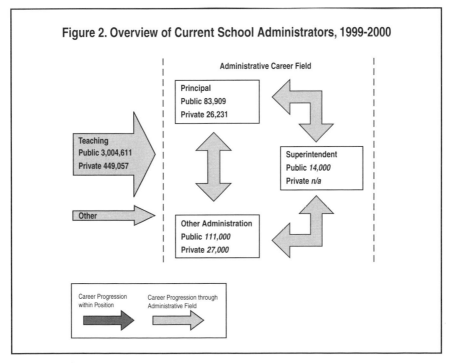

Figure 2. Overview of Current School Administrators, 1999-2000

Salary

Compensation has more than kept pace with inflation since 1987-88. After adjusting for changes in the consumer price index,[1] the average salary of public school principals increased by 9 percent, and the average salary of private school principals increased by nearly 40 percent since 1987-88. Despite the higher rate of salary growth in the private sector, public school principals still earn substantially more than private school principals (the average public school principal earns just over $65,000 per year, and the average private school principal earns more than $40,000 per year). The average salary of charter school principals is just under $54,000 and is substantially lower than the average public school salary of over $66,000.

The estimated average salary for all superintendents for 2000-01 was $118,811, and that increased to $121,794 in 2001-02. Adjusted for inflation, the average superintendent salary has increased by 14 percent since 1991-92 (Educational Research Service 2002). Salaries offered to superintendents of major urban school districts in 2000-01 ranged from $113,000 to $298,000, with an average of $165,144. In addition, most of the principals of major urban districts earned bonuses, pay-for-performance supplements, and other benefits with an average annual value of $44,954 per year (Council of Great City Schools 2001).

Other district-level administrators earn less than superintendents, but typically more than principals. The average salary of deputy or associate superintendents in 2001-02 was $104,048, and for assistant superintendents was $94,137. Average salaries for other administrators (e.g., finance and business, public relations, and staff services) ranged from $65,505 to $82,725.

Age and Experience

As indicated in Table 1, the average principal is in his or her late forties, and that average age increased slightly between 1988 and 2000—from 47.8 to 49.3 in the public sector and from 46 to 49.9 in the private sector.

These averages conceal the fact that the age distribution of principals in the public sector differs in interesting ways from the age distribution in the private sector. Whereas private school principals appear to be distributed fairly evenly across a wide age range from 35 to 65, a majority (53 percent) of public school principals fall in the 10-year window from 46 to 55 (see Gates et al. 2003). Another striking difference is that only a small proportion (17 percent) of public school principals are over age 55, compared with 27 percent of private school principals.

These differences in the age distributions between the public and private sectors suggest some potentially interesting differences in principal careers between the two sectors that would be worth exploring in greater detail. For example, private school principals may be more likely to enter the principalship at earlier ages and retire

Table 1. Description of All School Principals, 1999-2000

1999-2000	Public	Private
Number of principals*	83,909	26,231
Average age	49.3	49.9
Average annual salary**	$66,487	$41,656
Average years of principal experience	9.0	10.2
Average years of teaching experience	14.0	14.5
Percent women	43.7	54.6
Percent minority	17.8	11.1

Source: Department of Education Schools and Staffing Survey.
* Public school totals include charter schools and Bureau of Indian Affairs schools.
** Real 2000 dollars.

Table 2. Description of Charter School Principals

1999-2000	Charter
Number of principals	988
Average age	48.3
Average annual salary*	$53,920
Average years of principal experience	6.9
Average years of teaching experience	12.0
Percent women	54.0
Percent minority	29.4

Source: Department of Education Schools and Staffing Survey.
* Real 2000 dollars.

or leave the principalship later in life. Such differences would not be surprising, given differences in the retirement incentives of public relative to private school principals as well as differences in the recruitment strategies of private schools. It may also be that public principals are "retiring" into the private sector. Further exploration of these issues at the state and local levels could provide useful insights to policy makers.

Information on the distribution of principals' experience suggests that the increase in age among private but not public school principals stems from the tendency of people to stay on the job longer (see Gates et al. 2003). Private school principals are more experienced, whereas public school principals are now less experienced compared to 1988. Overall, the data suggest that principals are an aging population. Although the age increase is evident in both the public and private sectors, it appears to take different forms in the two sectors. Both public and private schools are hiring increasingly older new principals. In the public sector, principals tend not to remain in the principalship much beyond age 55, suggesting that those who enter the position later in life have shorter administrative careers. In the private sector, on the other hand, it is far more common for principals to stay on the job to age 60 or 65.

The 2000 survey of superintendents confirms that the administrative workforce is aging at this level of the career path as well. The median age of superintendents responding to the survey is 52.5—the oldest median age ever recorded in the survey, which is conducted approximately every 10 years. The increase in age is particularly striking in the smallest districts.[2] These individuals bring with them a good deal of experience in the superintendency—an average of 8.75 years (Glass et al. 2000). The average experience of superintendents is similar to the average tenure of CEOs, which was seven years in 2000 (Neff and Ogden 2001).

The corporate world appears to differ from the school administration career field in the age of senior managers. The average age of corporate CEOs declined from 59 in 1980 to 56 in 2000 (Neff and Ogden 2001).

Gender, Race and Ethnicity

The gender composition of principals has received substantial attention in the education literature amid concerns that the proportion of female principals is low relative to the proportion of female teachers (National Center for Education Statistics 1996; Bell and Chase 1993; Biklen and Brannigan 1980; Joy 1998; Riehl and Bird 1997). In 1999-2000, 56 percent of all public school principals were men (see table 1). This is down from 65 percent in 1993-94, and from 75 percent in 1987-88 (Gates et al. 2003). Women are well represented among charter school principals (see table 2). Men still comprise a majority of secondary school principals in both the public and the private sectors. As we noted earlier, high school principalships are the most highly-paid positions. Women now make up 55 percent of public elementary school principals, but just 21 percent of high school principals.

In private schools, women make up a majority of all elementary and combined school principals, and 38 percent of high school principals.

The representation of women in principal positions is substantially higher among new principals, defined as those with three or fewer years of principal experience. Considering only new public school principals, 54 percent are women. Well over half (60 percent) of the new principals in private schools are women.

Compared with the shift in the gender composition of school principals, changes in the racial mix have been more limited. Only a small proportion of principals are members of an ethnic or racial minority, particularly when compared with the proportion of minorities in the student population. Minority representation is higher in the public than in the private sector. Nearly 18 percent of public school principals are members of a racial or ethnic minority, compared with only

11 percent of private school principals (see Table 1). However, in charter schools, nearly 30 percent of principals are members of racial or ethnic minority groups (see Table 2).

We analyzed data to determine whether there is gender-based salary discrimination in school administration (Gates et al. 2003). The analysis examines the relationship between salary and school and individual characteristics of the principal, such as race, gender, and experience. We found that gender was not related to salary after controlling for other factors in the public sector, suggesting that females receive comparable pay for comparable work in the public sector. However, the private sector regression reveals that female private school principals earn nearly $6,000 per year less than their male counterparts after accounting for other factors. Race was not related to salary in either sector, except in the case of Native American principals, who earn nearly $3,000 per year less than White principals in public schools.[3] During the 1990s, female and minority representation increased among superintendents as well. An American Association of School Administrators' survey (Glass et al. 2000) indicates that women make up 13 percent of superintendents, double the proportion of superintendents who were women in the 1992 survey. According to this survey, 5.1 percent of superintendents are members of a racial or ethnic minority, and the number of minority superintendents increased by more than 30 percent since 1992. Minority superintendents are much better represented in the largest districts (those with enrollments over 25,000), where they account for 23 percent of all superintendents. Overall, the survey suggests that most minority superintendents serve in either large urban districts or in rural districts. Another survey of the superintendents of districts that are part of the Council of Great City Schools reveals that a majority of these superintendents are members of a racial or ethnic minority (37.5 percent African American and 14.3 percent Hispanic), and over 30 percent are female (Council of Great City Schools 2001).

Conclusions

Our review of existing research and analysis of data on school administrators reveals little evidence of a nationwide crisis in this market. Nevertheless, we do find issues with which policy makers might be concerned.

Aging Trends May Imply Shorter Careers

Overall, school administration appears to be a stable professional area experiencing neither tremendous growth nor tremendous decline. The national trends obscure some important regional variation, and high rates of growth in the number of school administrators suggest that strong demand might be putting pressure on labor markets in some western states.

Policy makers are greatly concerned about the impending retirement of a large proportion of current school administrators. Our analyses suggest that principals are indeed an aging group, but also indicate that the choices made by schools and districts in terms of hiring new principals, and the retirement programs themselves, may be contributing to this trend. Not only is the average age of principals increasing, but so is the average age of new principals. At the same time, the prevalence of principals over age 55 has not changed. Taken together, this implies that new principals have fewer years in the principalship before they reach retirement age. This is more of an issue in the public sector, where principals appear to be much less likely to remain on the job after age 55.

Although trends suggest new principals will have shorter careers, recent studies emphasize that schools and districts view administrative experience as a desirable quality and seek out experienced individuals to fill vacant positions.

Alternative Careers Are Neither More nor Less Attractive than Before

We find little evidence regarding a negative impact of labor market forces on the attractiveness of school administration as a career option. There is no evidence of high or increased rates of exit to suggest that people are being lured from school administration positions by other sectors of the economy. We also found little evidence to support the notion that there has been a change in the incentives for school administrators to leave the education career field in recent years. Comparing school administration with other options outside of education, we find no evidence that the real hourly wage of school administrators has changed relative to that of other professional managers over the 1983-1999 time period. Additionally, we see little evidence that school administrators are in fact leaving to take jobs in other sectors of the economy. Those who exit school administration typically exit the labor force entirely or return to teaching. On average, those leaving school administration experience a decrease in the average number of hours per week worked and in their average wage. Thus, school administrators apparently are not being lured away from their positions by high-paying private sector jobs.

Compensation Gap Is Shrinking

Although our analyses do not raise general concerns about the labor market conditions for school administrators, they do indicate that administrative salaries have increased more rapidly in private schools than in public schools over the last decade. As a result, it is possible that public schools may be facing greater competition for school administrators from private schools. A key question for policy makers is whether this change in the relative compensation has led more public school principals to move into the private sector. It is still true that public school principals earn substantially more than private school principals; however, we also know that private school principals report fewer problems in their schools than their public school counterparts. Our analyses suggest that movement of principals and administrators between the public and private sectors is uncommon, but does occur. As of 1994, there appeared to be a roughly equal transfer of principals and administrators between the private and public sectors, rather than a mass exodus from the public to the private sector. However, public school principals are slightly more likely to move to the private sector than vice-versa. We know that the average years of principal experience for current principals declined between 1988 and 2000 in public schools, but increased in private schools. Unfortunately, existing data do not allow us to examine trends in movement between the two sectors over time, or to specifically address the question of whether public school principals have become more likely in the past decade to leave for the private sector. Thus, although the evidence raises concerns, we cannot, at a national level, address the question of whether the narrowing in the salary gap between public and private school principals has made private school administration positions more attractive than positions in the public sector.

Teaching Is a Gateway to School Administration

Although there are many potential pathways to the principalship and superintendency, a vast majority of administrators begin their careers as teachers. Certainly, certification requirements play some role in the pervasiveness of this career pattern. However, the fact that nearly 90 percent of private school principals, who are not subject to state certification requirements, have served as teachers, suggests that such requirements are not the only reason schools tend to draw school administrators from the pool of teachers. There may be additional informal barriers embedded in the hiring process and the expectations of those reviewing resumes.

Because teaching is a gateway to school administration, it is crucial to understand the factors that encourage and deter teachers from moving into administrative positions. Certification requirements for administrators, which typically require certified teachers to obtain additional credits or degrees from an approved program, may pose a barrier to teachers as well as those outside the education field. Cultural barriers between managers and practitioners are common in organizations that rely on skilled technical professionals. Such organizations typically create a dual career track that develops career advancement opportunities for those who move into management as well as for those who don't make the move but develop into highly experienced practitioners. Other structural barriers may exist as well in the form of tenure and retirement systems.

A key issue is whether teachers have a financial incentive to move from teaching to school administration. Our analysis reveals that in general, the financial incentives do exist, although individual schools exist at which the incentives are weak or nonexistent. We find that public school principals earn 33 percent more than experienced teachers in their schools, and private school principals earn 44 percent more on an adjusted annual basis. Evidence does not exist to suggest that the magnitude of the pay differential is related to observable school characteristics in the public sector; in the private sector, principals of Catholic and other religiously affiliated schools receive less of a pay differential than principals of non-sectarian schools. Comparing the hourly wage of school administrators with that of teachers, we also find that educational administrators earn more.

Finally, it is worth pointing out that while teaching is the gateway to school administration, only a small fraction of teachers need to move into school administration in order to ensure an adequate supply. The number of school administrators is less than 10 percent of the number of teachers.

There is Little Evidence of Principal Sorting

Our analysis suggests that observable characteristics of a school can serve as a useful proxy for the degree of problems in the school. It also reveals that principals at the types of schools that tend to have more problems (e.g., larger, more diverse high schools) tend to earn more money as well.

One important exception exists to the consistency of the school problem-school characteristic-principal salary relationships. Principals in public schools with a larger fraction of students enrolled in the free and reduced-price lunch program earn *less* than their counterparts in schools with a smaller proportion of students enrolled in the program, even though such schools are perceived as "more problematic" by principals.

In spite of this disconnect between problems and salary paid to principals in schools with more low-income children, we find no evidence that such schools have principals with less experience. In other words, there is no evidence that principals are fleeing low-income schools for schools with fewer students enrolled in free and reduced-price lunch programs.

Our analysis of principal experience did not reveal any evidence of a tendency on the part of principals to move away from schools with certain observable characteristics as they gain more experience. In particular, we find no evidence that more experienced principals are systematically choosing to work in suburban schools, schools with smaller enrollments, or schools with a smaller proportion of minority, low-income, or LEP students.

We do find that, after controlling for observable school characteristics, principals in schools with more reported conflict problems have less experience. Although there is some relationship between principal reports of schools problems and observable school characteristics, there is additional variation in the perception of school conflict that is unexplained by the observable school characteristics.

At least two possible explanations exist for relationship between experience, school characteristics, and school problems descried here. First, it may be that the market for school principals is following the logic of the theory of compensating differentials, and the observed differences in salary offered in schools with different characteristics adequately compensate principals from the added difficulty of the job that can be explained by observable school characteristics. The fact that experienced principals are "sorting out" of schools with a high level of reported conflict problems could reflect the fact that observable school characteristics do a poor job predicting which schools have conflict problems, and hence compensation variation that is tied to observable school characteristics does not reward principals at conflict-ridden schools. Alternatively, it may be that principals are assigned to positions and do not in fact have more leverage to choose where they work as they gain more experience. Both explanations are inconsistent with the notion that there is a crisis in the ability of schools to attract and retain school principals.

Financial Incentives Differ by State

Overall, our analysis provides little evidence of a national crisis in school administration in terms of the characteristics of school administrators, movement into and out of administrative positions, or the incentives driving these moves. The results do reveal some important differences, however, across states in terms of the incentives principals face. Principals in some states fare well or poorly relative to other states in both absolute and relative salary, while in some states they fare well on one dimension and not so well on the other. In some states, such as Connecticut and New Jersey, principals are highly paid relative to principals in other states and also relative to teachers in their own state. In other states, such as Hawaii, North Carolina, the Dakotas, and Wyoming, principals are paid poorly relative to principals in other states, but are paid well relative to teachers in their own state. Another possibility, evident in Michigan, is that principals are paid well relative to principals in other states, but are paid poorly relative to teachers in their own state. Finally, in some states, such as West Virginia and Utah, principals are paid poorly both relative to principals in other states and relative to teachers in their own state. State policy makers may be interested in considering the results of this analysis in view of their own market conditions.

Individual Schools and Districts Face Challenges

Our analysis, which focused attention on national and state averages, and on systematic variation by school characteristic, suggests there is no national crisis, and indeed no crisis generally facing certain types of schools (e.g., urban, low-income, etc). At the same time, it is important to keep in mind that the data reveal a significant amount of local variation. More than 14,000 school districts and more than 100,000 schools exist in our country. In some of these schools and districts, principals are indeed earning less than experienced teachers in their schools. In some of these schools, the principals are in their first year on the job. Although we don't have data on school-level turnover, it is likely that some schools are experiencing frequent turnover. Our analysis, however, suggests that such problems are decidedly local in nature. For example, some urban, low-income schools are having trouble keeping experienced principals, while others succeed in retaining principals over a long period of time.

Recommendations

Although our analysis provides no evidence to support the notion of a nation-wide crisis in the ability of schools to attract and retain school administrators, it nevertheless raises some issues for policy makers and educational administrators to consider.

Trends in the age and experience distribution of school principals suggest that public schools are hiring people into the principalship at increasingly older ages, but that relatively few principals remain in these positions beyond age 55. If experience is a desired characteristic for school principals, then policy makers should consider policies and programs that could promote the entry of people into the principalship earlier in their career, keep them in the job beyond age 55, or both.

In view of recent increases in the compensation offered to private school administrators, the decline in the experience of public school principals and the increase in experience of private school principals, public policy makers should pay closer attention to the possible competition from the private sector. If possible, district administrators or state policy makers might try to identify a way to monitor movement of administrators between the public and private sectors and the relative salaries between the two sectors at a local and regional level. One issue that would be worth exploring in greater detail is the extent to which principals retire from the public sector at relatively early ages and take jobs in the private sector. A more in-depth exploration of the relative working conditions in the private versus the public sector may be worthwhile as well. Some argue that private school principals are paid less because they value the greater job flexibility they have relative to public school principals.

A richer understanding of public charter school principals might help policy makers understand the importance of such flexibility in attracting people into administrative positions. Charter school principals earn substantially less than their counterparts in other public schools. Forty-nine percent of charter school principals had been principals at other schools. Why are people willing to accept lower salaries at charter schools? Working conditions that relate to flexibility and control may be important to these individuals.

A key point of our analysis is that teaching is a gateway to school administration. For the most part, tomorrow's administrators are teachers today. This has several important implications for policy makers to consider. First, in order to attract high-quality administrators, high-quality potential administrators must be attracted into the teaching pool. Secondly, changes in the wages and working conditions of teachers can have an effect on the incentives teachers have to move into administration. The spillover effect of pay increases for teachers or class-size reductions should be kept in mind. Third, teaching is the fundamental activity going on in schools, and while schools need to develop some teachers into administrators, most teachers will remain in the classroom for their entire careers. A focus on school administration should not overlook a need to cultivate and reward experienced, expert teachers who remain in the classroom.

Finally, it is not clear whether the fact that teaching is a gateway to school administration is simply a self-fulfilling prophecy. Formal barriers such as certification requirements and informal barriers such as district hiring practices all but exclude those without teaching experience from consideration for administrative positions. If policy makers are serious about drawing people from outside education into school administration, those barriers must be addressed.

To the extent that there are problems in the market for school administrators, they are local and idiosyncratic in nature. This presents a challenge to policy makers because there is no easy target toward which to address solutions. Urban schools, low-income schools, or schools with a large number of English learners do not seem to be systematically having more trouble then rich, suburban schools in this labor market. If we had observed such systematic trends, crafting policy recommendations would be easier. Instead, the analysis suggests a need to closely monitor local market conditions and personnel management practices in order to craft target solutions. While the primary burden of such monitoring will fall on district administrators, the solutions to identified problems might require state-level intervention where an entire district cannot summon the resources to compete with neighboring districts or where a district fails to adequately monitor or respond to local labor market conditions.

Finally, although our analysis revealed no evidence that schools with a high fraction of low-income students are having trouble attracting and retaining experienced principals, the analysis of incentives suggests that this is an area for policy makers to monitor closely. Working conditions in such schools are harder, as measured by principal reports of school problems, and salaries are lower. Some schools and districts with a large proportion of low-income students may not have the resources to increase salaries in such a way as to attract principals by compensating them for more difficult working conditions. This is an issue that might need to be addressed at the state level.

Endnotes

1. To adjust the salary figures for different years, we used the CPI inflation adjustment calculator available at http://www.bls.gov/cpi/#overview.
2. The survey report divides districts into four categories based on district enrollment. Group A consists of districts with enrollments over 25,000; group B includes districts with enrollments between 3,000 and 24,999; group C includes those with enrollments between 300 and 2,999; and group D consists of districts with enrollments under 300 students.
3. This is a change from 1994, when Black principals earned nearly $1,800 per year more, and Hispanic principals earned $1,300 less than White principals. The difference between White and Native American principals was not significant.

References

Bell, C. & Chase, C. (1993). The underrepresentation of women in school leadership. In C. Marshall (Ed.), *The new politics of race and gender: The 1992 yearbook of the politics of education association* (pp. 140-154). London: Falmer.

Biklen, S. K. & Brannigan, M. (1980). *Women and educational leadership*. Lexington, MA: DC Health.

Colvin, R. (2000, June 28). A premium on principals. *Los Angeles Times.*

Council of Great City Schools (2001). *Urban school superintendents: Characteristics, tenure and salary third biennial survey.* Washington, DC: Council of Great City Schools. Retrieved from http://www.cgcs.org/reports/supers2001.PDF

Educational Research Service (2002). *Salaries and wages for professional and support personnel in public schools, 2001-2002.* Arlington, VA: Educational Research Service.

Gates, S. M., Ringel, J. S., Santibañez, L., Ross, K. E., & Chung, C. H. (2003). *Who Is leading our schools? An overview of school administrators and their careers.* Santa Monica, CA: RAND, MR-1697-EDU.

Glass, T., Bjork, L., & Brunner, C. (2000). *The study of the American school superintendency: A look at the superintendent of education in the new millennium.* Arlington, VA: American Association of School Administrators.

Joy, L. (1998). Why are women underrepresented in public school administration? An empirical test of promotion discrimination. *Economics of Education Review, 17*(2), 193-204.

National Center for Education Statistics (1996). *Teachers' working conditions. Findings from The condition of education, 1996.* Washington, DC: U.S. Department of Education, Office of Educational Research and Improvement.

Neff, T. & Ogden, D. (2001, February). Anatomy of a CEO. *Chief Executive.* Retrieved from http://www.chiefexecutive.net/depts/routetop/anatomyofaceo.html

Riehl, C. & Byrd, M. (1997). Gender differences among new recruits to school administration: Cautionary footnotes to an optimistic tale. *Educational Evaluation and Policy Analysis, 19*(1), 45-64.

Susan M. Gates, Ph.D., is an economist currently leading a project funded by the Wallace-Reader's Digest Funds on the career paths of principals and superintendents. Jeanne S. Ringel, Ph.D., is an economist, and Lucrecia Santibañez, Ph.D., is an associate economist, both at RAND. Abigail Brown is a Research Fellow at the Pardee Rand Graduate School and is pursuing her Ph.D. studies in Policy Analysis.

Chapter 10: Questions for Reflection and Discussion

1. This chapter discusses a RAND Corporation study that addressed three overall questions about school administrator careers. Based on your experience and observations, how would you answer the following questions:

   • What would you describe as the general characteristics of school administrators? How have they changed over time?

   • What factors contribute to the entry and exit decisions of professionals moving into and out of administration?

2. The study found that the majority of school administrators began their careers as teachers. What was your career path? Do you feel that administrators with teaching experience are at an advantage? Why or why not?

3. The author discusses the ability of a school to attract and retain school administrators. What incentives do you feel would be attractive to potential school administrators?

Index

A

Administrators

    Characteristics—47, 49, 56, 85, 99, 121, 127, 128, 130, 135

    District—14, 15, 17, 140, 141

    Knowledge—3, 4, 5, 6, 7, 10, 11, 17, 23, 24, 25, 26, 27, 28, 29, 30, 31, 33, 35, 36, 37, 38, 39, 40, 42, 43, 44, 46, 47, 49, 59, 62, 67, 71, 72, 75, 76, 77, 80, 81, 82, 87, 88, 89, 96

    Preparation Programs—6, 24, 28, 31, 87, 88, 89, 91, 93, 96, 98, 128

    School—10, 24, 31, 36, 87, 88, 89, 91, 94, 95, 115, 127, 128, 129, 130, 131, 135, 136, 137, 138, 139, 140, 141, 142, 143

    Stress—97, 98, 99, 100, 101, 102, 103, 104, 105, 106, 107, 108, 109, 110, 111, 112, 113, 114, 115, 116, 117

Assessments

    High-Stakes—7, 23, 36, 44, 81

    Statewide—22, 100, 101

C

Careers—127, 128, 129, 130, 132, 134, 135, 136, 137, 141, 142, 143

Collaboration—10, 44, 59, 62, 94

Curriculum—3, 4, 5, 7, 14, 20, 21, 26, 31, 35, 45, 46, 47, 48, 49, 50, 59, 61, 62, 63, 64, 65, 66, 67, 77, 79, 80, 84, 123

D

Discipline—38, 43, 77, 105, 106, 107, 108, 109, 110, 111, 112, 113, 114, 117, 124

ERS Subscriptions at a Glance

If you are looking for reliable preK-12 research to ...

- tackle the challenges of NCLB

- identify research-based teaching practices

- make educationally sound and cost-effective decisions, and most importantly

- improve student achievement ...

then look no further than an ERS Subscription.

Simply pick the subscription option that best meets your needs:

■ **School District Subscription**—a special research and information subscription that provides education leaders with timely research on priority issues in preK-12 education. All new ERS publications and periodicals, access to customized information services through the ERS special library, and 50 percent discounts on additional ERS resources are included in this subscription for one annual fee. This subscription also provides the entire administrative staff "instant" online, searchable access to the wide variety of ERS resources. You'll gain access to the ERS e-Knowledge Portal of more than 1,600 educational research-based documents, as well as additional content uploaded throughout the year.

■ **Individual Subscription**—designed primarily for school administrators, staff, and school board members who want to receive a personal copy of new ERS studies, reports, and/or periodicals published and special discounts on other resources purchased.

■ **Other Education Agency Subscription**—available for state associations, libraries, departments of education, service centers, and other organizations needing access to quality research and information resources and services.

Your ERS Subscription benefits begin as soon as your order is received and continue for 12 months. For more detailed subscription information and pricing, contact ERS toll free at 800-791-9308, by email at ers@ers.org, or visit us online at www.ers.org!

ORDER FORM FOR RELATED RESOURCES

ERS

Quantity	Item Number	Title	Base Price	ERS Individual Subscriber Discount Price	ERS School District Subscriber Discount Price	Total Price
				Price per Item		
	0407	*Essentials for Principals: How to Interview, Hire, and Retain High-Quality New Teachers*	$25.95	$19.46	$12.98	
	0444	*Essentials for Principals: Effective Teacher Observations*	$25.95	$19.46	$12.98	
	0490	*What Principals Need to Know About Teaching: Differentiated Instruction*	$25.95	$19.46	$12.98	
		Postage and Handling** (Add the greater of $4.50 or 10% of purchase price.)				
		Express Delivery** (Add $20 for second-business-day service.)				
		**Please double for international orders.			TOTAL PRICE:	

> **SATISFACTION GUARANTEED! If you are not satisfied with an ERS resource, return it in its original condition within 30 days of receipt and we will give you a full refund.**

Visit us online at www.ers.org for a complete listing of resources!

Method of payment:

☐ Check enclosed (payable to ERS) ☐ P.O. enclosed (Purchase order # _____)

☐ MasterCard   ☐ VISA   ☐ American Express

Name on Card: _____ Credit Card #: _____

Expiration Date: _____ Signature: _____

Ship to: (please print or type)   ☐ Dr.   ☐ Mr.   ☐ Mrs.   ☐ Ms.

Name: _____ Position: _____

School District or Agency: _____ ERS Subscriber ID#: _____

Street Address: _____

City, State, Zip: _____

Telephone: _____ Fax: _____

Email: _____

Return completed order form to:
Educational Research Service 1001 North Fairfax Street, Suite 500 • Alexandria, VA 22314
Phone: (703) 243-2100 • Toll Free Phone: (800) 791-9308 • Fax: (703) 243-1985 • Toll Free Fax: (800) 791-9309
Email: ers@ers.org • Web site: www.ers.org